"Most of us do everything in our power to avoid
Meanwhile, adversity is God's primary tool for helpi
develop spiritual maturity. In this powerful book, F
various forms of adversity we all face. She offers many
as her riveting personal testimony, to show us how to draw near to God when
life is difficult—and how to let God use adversity to strengthen us. This is a book
of hope, healing, and encouragement for all of life's trials."

> —**Stacey Pardoe**, author of *Lean Into Grace: Let God Heal Your Heart, Restore Your Soul, and Set You Free*; coauthor of *Girl to Girl: 60 Mother-Daughter Devotions for a Closer Relationship and Deeper Faith*; and writer at staceypardoe.com

"*Draw Near* is a beautifully written and inspiring devotional. Hadassah Treu cleverly and clearly outlines thirteen gifts God uses to help us live courageously while facing struggles and growing in our faith. Hadassah creates a safe space to authentically explore your suffering using Scripture, Biblical characters and her own experiences. *Draw Near* is a must read for anyone seeking comfort and strength in the midst of suffering."

> —**Mary Rooney Armand**, author of *Identity, Understanding, and Accepting Who I am in Christ* and *Life Changing Stories: A Devotional Collection Revealing God's Faithfulness and Transforming Power*, life coach and creator of ButterflyLiving.org

"If you've walked the tumultuous path of anxiety, this book feels like a gentle hand reaching out. It beautifully captures the raw essence of this struggle, offering not just empathy, but a roadmap to transformation. The wisdom within these pages reminds us that surrendering these fears to God is not weakness, but the truest form of strength. If you're navigating the turbulent waters of anxiety, this book will be your beacon of hope."

> —**Landen Melton**, creator and founder of Devotable: Daily Christian Devotion, podcaster, editor, and publisher of *Extinguishing the Spirit of Fear*, *Equality: Created Equal in His Image*, *Perseverance* and *Prayer: Approaching the Throne of Grace*

"This book is an engaging, heartfelt example of the wisdom contained in 2 Corinthians 1:3- 4, "Praise be to God...who comforts us in all our troubles, so that we can comfort those in any trouble." With a balanced blend of memoir, Bible study, and self-help, Hadassah Treu reminds us that God is at work in every trial. *Draw Near* is a must-read for any Christian who is seeking spiritual gain after a season of loss."

> —**Sarah Koontz**, Founder of Living by Design Ministries

"Hadassah's writing reminds us that our deepest sufferings also hold beautifully wrapped gifts from God. Her ability to empathize with our trials while encouraging us to believe God remains faithful in our circumstances helps us take the next step forward on our healing journey."

> —**Angie Baughman**, author of *Strong Hearts, A Journey Worth Taking*, pastor, Bible teacher, founder of Steady On ministries, and creator of the Step By Step Bible study method

"Yes, life hurts beyond what we ever expected. Hadassah's book, *Draw Near*, reminds readers that God is always present to provide comfort and strength if we turn towards Him. This inspiring book will give readers a new perspective on their pain as they uncover the gifts wrapped up in their losses. *Draw Near* is sure to be a book readers come back to again and again for encouragement and hope."

> —**Maree Dee**, founder of Embracing the Unexpected Ministries, a writer, speaker, and mental health coach

"In *Draw Near: How Painful Experiences Become Birthplace of Blessings*, Hadassah reveals the role that suffering plays in our spiritual maturation and preparation. Listing thirteen primary afflictions encountered in this life, she uncovers the underlying losses for each suffering experienced to reveal spiritual gains. Interpreting suffering as a gift through the word of God, Hadassah removes the roadblocks to God that suffering can often yield, paving the way to draw near to God through suffering rather than around it."

> —**Denise Pass**, M.A. Biblical Exposition, Author of *Make Up Your Mind* and *Shame Off You*, speaker and founder, Seeing Deep Ministries

"You don't have to be a mathematical genius to know that the equation "five minus four equals one" is correct. But in God's economy, "five minus four" can equate to five, seven, ten or an infinite number of possibilities. In her book, *Draw Near*, Hadassah Treu demonstrates the truth of this statement and invites her readers to draw near to God as they navigate through their adversities and sufferings in life. She inspires them to look at their difficult seasons through God's lenses. With this fresh perspective, they will discover that Yahweh Yireh–"The Lord Will Provide," bestows them with gains that far outweigh their losses from these trying experiences. If you are going through trials or a challenging season, I invite you to let the pages of this book assist you in finding tokens of God's gifts buried in the mathematical equations of life."

—**Cecille Valoria**, author of *Slaying Your Fear Giants*, speaker, and Digging Deep for Treasures Podcast host

"Hadassah has the most beautiful way of articulating deep spiritual healing. In this book, she eloquently takes the reader through the transformation necessary for a godly perspective shift. Hadassah shows the positive plans for growth that God has deposited in even the worst of seasons. How she unpacks God's truth and faithfulness in all situations brings hope and revelation! I highly recommend this book for all who sojourn through our often difficult world. Be open to God's leading and allow Him to transform you!"

—**Amanda Schaefer**, author of *Crumbled: A Place for Broken People*, speaker, A Cup of Gratitude podcast host

"With great candor and kind compassion, Hadassah Treu has penned a transforming balm of hope for the hurting heart. *Draw Near* is a loving invitation to release pain for gain—to let go, yes, of the pain of any life loss for the gain that God plants into our desperate teardrops. A remarkable blend of devotional, Bible study, and storytelling, this gentle guide will help the wounded move from the struggle to control to the sweet gift of God's comfort and strength. It's a healing oil of love for wounded souls."

—**Patricia Raybon**, Christy Award-winning author of *God Is Our Help* from Our Daily Bread Publishing and the *Annalee Spain Mysteries* from Tyndale Fiction

"*Draw Near* by Hadassah Treu is a compelling exploration of the transformative power of adversity. She skillfully intertwines personal experience with profound insights, illustrating how embracing challenges, much like our everyday lives lead to spiritual growth. Hadassah weaves a tapestry of wisdom, guiding readers through the layers of hardship she faced with a deep understanding of how adversity further shapes and forms God's plan and purpose for our lives. I appreciate how through the lens of Psalm 84:5-7, she illustrates the potential for strength and resilience gained when faced with challenges of adversity but also unveils the hidden treasures it offers; character transformation, an intimate relationship with Christ, and a profound sense of joy independent of circumstances. Ms. Treu's insights, grounded in biblical wisdom and truth, provide readers with invaluable keys of navigating adversity with grace, purpose, acceptance and gratitude. *Draw Near* is a thought-provoking journey that keeps the reader engaged, inspiring resilience and spiritual maturity."

—**Dr. LaVonda McCullough**, CPQC, D. Div., Christian life coach, founder of Joyful Journey LLC

"In our darkest moments, it's often easy to question God's love and care. And yet, Jesus wants to meet us in the midst of our deepest sorrows in order to show us what we can gain in Him. *Draw Near* is a beautiful testimony of God's ability to redeem any hardship we may face. Hadassah offers biblical wisdom, encouragement, and truth based on her own experience with loss that's relatable and authentic. She invites us to lean into Christ when life is difficult and receive unfailing hope our hurting hearts need. I'm so grateful for this life-giving message."

—**Becky Beresford**, Speaker, Coach and Author of *She Believed HE Could, So She Did*

"If you are looking for hope and encouragement in the ups and downs of your life, this book has practical help for you. Hadassah Treu wisely and compassionately shows you the gains and losses in many trials you face, and points you back to God's lovingkindness. Reading it is like having a thoughtful conversation with a good friend."

—**Sarah Geringer**, author of seven books, speaker, editor, artist, creative coach, and book launch manager at sarahgeringer.com

"What if the seasons of our greatest adversity were places of our deepest growth with God? In *Draw Near*, Hadassah Treu shows how the pain of a traumatic childhood, infertility, rejection, and becoming a widow were catalysts to help her find hope and healing in Christ. Hadassah takes us through a scripture-saturated journey to help us see life's difficulties as gifts and suffering as an opportunity to draw closer to God."

—**Lisa Appelo**, author of *Life Can Be Good Again: Putting Your World Back Together After It All Falls Apart*

Hadassah Treu

Draw Near

How Painful Experiences Become the Birthplace of Blessings

HADASSAH TREU

CALLA PRESS
PUBLISHING

Draw Near

Draw Near: How Painful Experiences Become the Birthplace of Blessings
Copyright @ 2024 by Hadassah Treu
Published by Calla Press Publishing
       Texas Countryside
       United States 76401

All rights reserved. No part of this publication may be reproduced, stored in a retrieval system or transmitted in any form by any means electronic, mechanical, photocopy, recording, or otherwise without the prior permission of the publisher, except as provided by USA copyright law.

Cover Design: Publisher of Calla Press Publishing
First Printing, 2024
Printed in the United States of America

Unless otherwise indicated, Scripture quotations are from THE HOLY BIBLE, NEW INTERNATIONAL VERSION®, NIV® Copyright @ 1973, 1978, 1984, 2011 by Biblica, Inc.® Used by permission. All rights reserved worldwide.
All emphases in Scripture quotations have been added by the author.

Trade paperback ISBN: 979-8-9888702-1-0
e-book ISBN: 979-8-9888702-2-7

Hadassah Treu

For Thomas.

*Celebrating the precious gifts of your life and your love;
your fierce belief in me and your unwavering support.
My pains were your pains, and my gains were your gains.*

I love you, always.

Draw Near

Table of Contents

Foreword — 1

Introduction — 3

1. The Gifts Hidden in Adversity — 6
2. The Gifts Hidden in Sadness — 18
3. The Gifts Hidden in Anxiety — 30
4. The Gifts Hidden in Rejection — 40
5. The Gifts Hidden in Loneliness — 52
6. The Gifts Hidden in Unmet Expectations — 63
7. The Gifts Hidden in Disillusionment — 74
8. The Gifts Hidden in Grief — 85
9. The Gifts Hidden in Betrayal — 97
10. The Gifts Hidden in Broken Dreams — 108
11. The Gifts Hidden in Hopelessness — 119
12. The Gifts Hidden in Failure — 130
13. The Gifts Hidden in Pain — 141

Summary of Declarations — 152

A Request from the Author — 158

Acknowledgments — 159

About the Author — 161

Draw Near

Foreword

"How do I do this?"

I was sitting in a chair in the front row at my father's graveside service. I thought my life was over. I was 15, grew up in an environment of mixed messages, sexual abuse, and mental illness. Both my grandfathers died before I was six. I was bullied at school, was painfully shy, and spoke to almost no one. I lost a good friend at the age of 12, my parents divorced, and mother attempted suicide. If life wasn't already dark, my dad collapsed and died in front of me.

As I sat in that chair staring at my father's grave, I wondered, *Is this what life is? What do I do now?*

"How do I do this?" is a question we face often in life. We ask ourselves this question in some shape, form, or fashion multiple times every day–perhaps even every hour. Many times, the answer to this question is obvious and easy. Other times, the answer seems to elude us, especially when it comes to the tougher things in life–things like disappointment, rejection, personal pain, and loss.

This world is not a friendly place. We face challenge after challenge, difficulty after difficulty. Our hearts get hit over and over again with things like: adversity, sadness, anxiety, rejection, loneliness, unmet expectations, grief, disillusionment, betrayal, broken dreams, hopelessness, failure, and pain.

This persistent avalanche of hardship can be crushing. We grow tired and weary. We begin going through the motions. We somehow manage to smile at times, but we're screaming inside.

We find ourselves asking on a much deeper level, "How do I do this?"

And that, my friends, is what this book is all about.

In the following pages, Hadassah has given us the road map to healing. All healing ultimately comes from Jesus Christ Himself and *Draw Near* points us directly to Him.

Each chapter contains valuable insights drawn from Scripture and personal experiences on how to walk with Jesus through difficulty and suffering. The affirmations, reflection questions, suggested meditation verses, and prayer at the end of each chapter are incredibly practical.

In other words, *Draw Near* helps us answer that important question, "How do I do this?"

I can honestly say that I wish I had this book decades ago.

Draw Near puts words to our silent suffering and turns our attention to God who continually takes disaster and pain and uses it for our good and the good of those around us.

However, *Draw Near* is ultimately not about suffering. This book is about victory. These pages are about overcoming and living out our identity in Christ. We are truly more than conquerors in Him.

I encourage you to take your time with this book. Please don't get in a hurry, read at God's pace for you, and let the Lord work in you. Focus on *drawing near*.

Thank you, Hadassah, for such a wonderful resource.

May the Lord bless and guide you as you read.

–*Gary Roe*, Amazon best-selling and multiple award-winning author, speaker, and grief specialist

Introduction

I want you to meet Susan.

Susan is a middle-aged woman living with her husband and two children: one young adult and one teenager. She works as a librarian and she loves reading books and meeting her friends in the coffee shop or for a walk in nature. She loves having fellowship with other women in her Bible Study group and enjoys taking part in Christian conferences. Susan is a devout Christian who wants to grow and mature in Christ. She enjoys reading Christian nonfiction books, devotionals, and Bible Studies that teach about Christian spiritual growth, Christian living, memoirs, and biographies.

She loves fixer-upper shows and make-over shows in which the ugly duck turns into a swan. Such stories move her to tears. She loves fantasy and science fiction stories in which in the end the good triumphs and the hero has gone through a remarkable transformation.

Susan wanted to become a doctor when she was a child, but she could not afford this kind of education. However, her inclination to help people in various ways stayed. She is a faithful friend and has a listening ear. Often, she finds it difficult to resist her people-pleasing tendencies and to set boundaries.

She has a good relationship with her husband, although there were several challenging seasons in their marriage. She worries a lot about her teenage daughter and the poor choices she makes. Susan had several traumatic experiences in the last ten years that left her reeling back and shook the foundations of her faith. She lost her brother in a car accident five years ago and soon after that, her mother passed away.

Her best friend put an end to their friendship with no explanation. Soon after that, Susan experienced her first panic attack and was diagnosed with an anxiety disorder. These painful experiences and ongoing struggles have left Susan wounded and hurting. She struggles to reconcile the pain she feels and the trauma she has gone through with God's goodness. Often she doesn't understand, and she can't find satisfying answers to her questions.

Why me? Why this? Why now? How am I going to heal from this pain? Where are you, Lord?

These are the questions she often asks when she lays awake in the night, with tears burning down her cheeks. She needs a new perspective, a deeper understanding, and the assurance of God's love and good plans in her painful experiences. She longs for comfort and hope. Susan strives to see God's intentions and purpose in her darkness. She wants to gain understanding and fix her eyes on the divine transformation going on in her heart; she needs to believe in the metamorphosis God is weaving out; she longs to see and embrace meaning and purpose in her suffering.

Do you face the same struggles as Susan?

We all do. We all need a biblical perspective and a new look at suffering to help us reconcile our painful experiences with what we know about God. Suffering remains a mystery and there is no simple theological answer to it. But what is our role? What are we supposed to think and do when we go through undeserved and unexpected pain and trauma?

The first and most important is to learn to see our dark moments as new chances and opportunities to draw near to God. We can choose to take off the glasses of loss and replace them with the lenses of God's love, biblical truths, and thankfulness. Then our outlook will change and we will see more of the bigger picture. We can choose to live with open minds, believing God's Word, with hands raised in prayer. We can commit to putting every effort into finding the balance between the reality we live in and the reality in which we live with God. It is in this balance of our reality and God's reality that we find peace instead of fear, rest instead of anxiety, and wholeness instead of destruction.

Our painful experiences are glorious opportunities to draw near to God, to bond with Him, and to enjoy intimacy and fellowship with Him amidst the pain. This is the most important thing we can do in our lives because everything else results from bonding and connection. A loving connection with God births maturity, growth, transformation, and eternal blessings. Besides that, suffering is a privilege and a possibility to take part in our Lord's sufferings and to know the power of His resurrection.

"I want to know Christ—yes, to know the power of his resurrection and participation in his sufferings, becoming like him in his death" (Phil. 3:10). Our painful experiences are a golden path: a path to self-knowledge and God-knowledge. We learn to know our true selves through our emotions and we experience more of God's power, comfort, guidance, and grace in our pain. He communes with us and He delivers us from our pain and suffering. "But those who suffer he delivers in their suffering; he speaks to them in their affliction" (Job 36:15).

Suffering is also often one of God's most used ways to humble us and prepare us for ministry and service. In this way, we become not only blessing recipients, but blessing-givers.

Are you marked by pain and suffering? Know that you are also marked for ministry, service, and to bless others. When we choose to listen and draw near to God in our pains, something miraculous will happen. God's Spirit will birth blessings and precious gifts out of the pain.

Are you ready to unpack them?

1

The Gifts Hidden in Adversity

When my trainer in the gym suggested I increase the weights in the exercises for my arms, I thought, "It's impossible to lift this weight and complete three series." But I tried it. At first, it surprised me I could lift this additional weight, and that I could make 15 repetitions. My muscles burned with pain; I was panting while sweat drops covered my face. I thought this was torture. However, after several weeks of using this weight, my muscles got accustomed, and I was ready for the next level. My trainer explained this training principle the following way: for the muscles to stay in shape and to grow, they need to be "stressed" and exposed to increasing pressure. True.

I often think about our faith muscles and how God allows different adversities in our lives to "stress" and press them to strengthen us and make us healthier and more resilient. The aim is to grow spiritually, become mature, and be able to carry heavier loads without breaking. This is all part of God's special preparation and training for his kingdom.

Nobody likes the pain and pressure of adversity. But what exactly is adversity? According to the Merriam-Webster dictionary, adversity is, "a state or instance of serious or continued difficulty or misfortune."[1] Synonyms of adversity include misfortune, bad luck, trouble, difficulty, hardship, and distress. The Bible dictionary defines adversity as the various forms of distress and evil conveyed by four Hebrew words: *tsela*ʾ, "a halting" or "fall"; *tsarah*, "straits" "distress," "affliction"; *tsar*, "straitness," "affliction"; *ra*ʾ, "bad," "evil," "harmful." These words cover the entire range of misfortunes caused by enemies, poverty, sorrow, and trouble.[2]

We can say that every kind of difficulty and distress is adversity. This means that we struggle with adversity every single day. Every day has its share of evil. These may be smaller evils like technical problems at work, stress with the boss, or family inconveniences. There may be more serious afflictions like illness, dysfunctional relationships, financial strains, and struggles with mental illness. Some adversities are just for a day or a week; others continue for months or even years and have a profound impact on shaping our characters. Adversity is the primary training tool in God's training arsenal.

I have encountered many adversities in my life as a believer, including minor and more serious ones. One of the biggest adversities I have struggled with for many years was infertility. It felt like a heavy burden, nearly impossible to carry every day. This was a source of constant emotional pain and suffering that expressed itself in my body as anxiety, panic attacks, muscle pain, and stomach pain. I experienced the pressure and the stress of this adverse situation for at least five years. But those five years were also some of the most fruitful spiritual formation years of my life.

The Losses of Comfort and Happiness

When we are in a difficult situation, the first loss we experience is that of our comfort and ease. Hardship forces us out of our comfort zones; it stretches and challenges us. Life becomes

---

[1] https://www.merriam-webster.com/dictionary/adversity
[2] https://www.biblestudytools.com/dictionary/adversity/

difficult and burdensome. However, in the place of our discomfort, we start to gain new strength and resilience. We start to grow and gain maturity. Overcoming difficulties produces a quality change in us: a character transformation, beautifully described in this verse, "Blessed are those whose strength is in you, whose hearts are set on pilgrimage. As they pass through the Valley of Baka, they make it a place of springs; the autumn rains also cover it with pools. They go from strength to strength, till each appears before God in Zion" (Ps. 84:5-7).

We also lose our happiness and satisfaction, at least the happiness tied to our circumstances. But this gives us a chance to experience another type of happiness and find another kind of satisfaction. We have our most powerful key to happiness and satisfaction in our relationship with Christ. Through Christ, God invites us to enter a relationship with him in which he shows us his love: a love that floods the deserts in our hearts and makes us capable to, in our turn, love as God loves us.

Happiness and satisfaction, not based on our circumstances, are one of the greatest gains of adversity. There are three biblical keys to happiness and contentment in times of adversity: the key to acceptance, the key to gratitude, and the key to the right motivation. During adversity, we learn to accept our imperfect life as it is, not as we want it—a tangle of pain and joy. We learn to surrender it in all its imperfections and brokenness to God, to his care and guidance, and to live with the awareness that he holds all these broken pieces and makes them full of life.

Experiencing the presence and the love of God during our hardships also changes our motivation about what we do and how we work. This love compels us to do our best and to put every effort into what we do. Not for human praise, nor money, but as before the Lord and unto the Lord; "Obey them not only to win their favor when their eye is on you, but as slaves of Christ, doing the will of God from your heart. Serve wholeheartedly, as if you were serving the Lord, not people" (Eph. 6:6-7). By working as to the Lord, we increase the quality of everything that comes out of our hands, either in work or in our private life. This way, we contribute both to our own happiness and satisfaction and bring joy to others who benefit from our work.

Finally, adversity teaches us to make God and his love our greatest source of satisfaction in every situation and season of life.

The Role of Our Expectations

Another serious loss we experience when we encounter hardships and distress connects to our expectations. To our suffering, we add more struggles. Struggles that contain unmet expectations: unfulfilled plans, wishes, and dreams. This can be extremely painful, leading to a permanent state of disappointment and discouragement. During my struggle with infertility, my unmet expectations and unfulfilled desire to become a mother were a constant thorn in the flesh—a source of intense emotional and even physical pain and mental distress.

Everybody knows how an unmet expectation feels: an explosive mixture of disappointment, discontent, pain, anger, insecurity, and doubt. Unmet expectations can make us doubt God's love and his good intentions. Questions like, *Does God even care about my desires, Does he really want to bless me, Does he really see the dreams of my heart,* spread sticky nets of doubt that erode our trust and diminish our hope. If we leave these responses unaddressed and unprocessed, we risk falling into a constant state of discouragement and negativity.

Our logic is simple. If God loves us, he would care about our desires and expectations, and he would bless us by giving us what we expect. Mind you, we talk about good things here: a well-paying job, good health, a happy marriage, a faithful and caring husband, children, good friends, satisfying relationships, a long life, a fair treat, and the list goes on.

Can I share a secret with you, friend?

Many of these expectations will not come true. But this has nothing to do with God not loving us or not wanting to bless us. Quite the opposite—God has buried precious lessons and blessings in unmet expectations. Unmet expectations propel us closer to God and enable us "to grasp how wide and long and high and deep is the love of Christ" (Eph. 3:18). There are depths of God's love and grace that we can only experience when we swim in the bitter waters of adversity, disappointment, and loss. It is in these dark, cold waters that God moves even closer. In the darkness, he lets us experience the inexpressible comfort of his presence. It is there that we learn his presence is enough. When our hopes for things and people in this life grow weak, then God offers us a greater hope that doesn't disappoint. This is the hope of the renewal of all things, of everything made right, of "a new heaven and a new earth, where righteousness dwells" (2 Pet. 3:13).

Every unmet expectation is an opportunity to grow roots in this glorious hope and to invest our deepest longings into it. These blessings and gains of unmet expectations belong to the process of spiritual growth, preparing us for the splendorous future of being God's beloved.

Let's now take a look at two biblical heroes and their stories, that illustrate the need and the principle of spiritual growth and preparation through adversity.

Losses and Gains in the Story of Joseph

Joseph is one of my favorite biblical heroes. We find Joseph's story in Genesis 37:2–50:26. Joseph was the favorite son of Jacob, born to him by his wife, Rachel. As a teenager, Joseph had a prophetic dream that he would rise to a position of leadership and all his brothers would bow to him. This dream provoked his brothers into hatred and jealousy. They sold him as a slave and he ended up in Egypt in the house of Potiphar. This was the beginning of a 13-year dark period in Joseph's life, full of various kinds of adversity.

In the house of Potiphar, Joseph faced the next adversity: the schemes of Potiphar's wife, who wanted to make him her lover. However, Joseph kept his integrity and constantly refused her. Infuriated, she accused him falsely and he ended up in prison for something he hadn't done.

A pit, slavery, false accusation, prison—the pressure on Joseph increased. There was a glimpse of hope in the prison when Joseph interpreted the dreams of two of Pharaoh's officials. One of the officials regained his former position, just as Joseph had interpreted, but he forgot about Joseph right away. This was another kind of adversity and evil that Joseph needed to face.

Two more years passed until Joseph gained an opportunity to be released from his misery in prison, by interpreting Pharaoh's disturbing dreams that no one could interpret. Joseph testified to God's ability to provide these interpretations and gave all glory to God. God's presence with Joseph was so obvious that Pharaoh promoted Joseph to second-in-command of Egypt, specifically to take charge of preparations for the coming famine.

Joseph lost a lot in these long years of adversity. He lost his freedom and to a certain extent, his trust in people: first, in his brothers, then in his masters, and then in the person whom he helped in prison. Of course, he also lost his comfort and privileged position in his father's house. Because of his dire circumstances, he lost his happiness as well.

In these 13 years of suffering, he probably thought that there was no way his prophetic dream would come to pass. The tragic events in his life extinguished his plans, expectations, and wishes to become a leader. These severe adversities brought many heavy losses to Joseph, but let's also look at his *gains*. The most important gain for Joseph was that God's presence was with him. It was sustaining, preserving, and transforming him. When he resisted the sexual harassment attempts of Potiphar's wife, Joseph gained strength of character and integrity. He learned how to say "no" and resist temptation.

According to Genesis 39:21-23, Joseph's stay in prison was marked by the Lord's presence, the jailer's favor, and Joseph's promotion to a position of leadership. Joseph learned patience, humility, and long-suffering by the time when the Pharaoh finally promoted him. At that point, he was already another man, mature and ready to act as a leader. The adversity didn't harden his heart. Instead, his heart got softer and more forgiving, enabling him to forgive his brothers when they came to Egypt in search of food. The adversity and God's presence forged another person, completely capable of being the leader the nation needed.

Like Joseph, when we face various adversities and afflictions, we may struggle to understand and accept our lot in life, but Psalm 16 gives us a more accurate and beautiful perspective, "Lord, you alone are my portion and my cup; you make my lot secure. The boundary lines have fallen for me in pleasant places; surely I have a delightful inheritance" (Ps. 16:5-6).

Each one who is in Christ has a secure lot, boundaries in pleasant places, and a delightful inheritance. These places may and will involve adversity, heartaches, loss, and things we want to avoid. Yet at the same time, include a portion of God's presence, love, gladness, peace, and joy. It is exactly amidst our struggles that we experience our share of God's abundant grace, provision, and power. We receive our portion of adversity in our lives, but this is a portion packed with God's presence that permeates and transforms every pain and difficulty. This is, and always will be, our greatest gain.

The Effect of Adversity in the Life of Apostle Paul

We have another example of the effect of adversity in the life of a great biblical hero from the New Testament: the Apostle Paul. His conversion to Christianity was dramatic and brought him the temporary loss of his eyesight. He didn't only get struck blind on the road to Damascus, but lost his confidence in his previous life and in everything he knew and was. However, all these losses were necessary so he could gain the most important thing in life: a relationship and a new life with Christ (Acts 9:1-19). Paul began his new life as an apostle, evangelist, and missionary. We may think that as an apostle of Christ, he had a wonderful life, but in fact, his life was full of adversity, opposition, and hardships. Here is how he defends his apostleship in the second Epistle to the Corinthians:

> "Are they servants of Christ? (I am out of my mind to talk like this.) I am more. I have worked much harder, been in prison more frequently, been flogged more severely, and been exposed to death again and again. Five times I received from the Jews the forty lashes minus one. Three times I was beaten with rods, once I was pelted with stones, three times I was shipwrecked, I spent a night and a day in the open sea, I have been constantly on the move. I have been in danger from rivers, in danger from bandits, in danger from my fellow Jews, in danger from Gentiles; in danger in the city, in danger in the country, in danger at sea; and in danger from false believers. I have labored and toiled and have often gone without sleep; I have known hunger and thirst and have often gone without food; I have been cold and naked. Besides everything else, I face daily the pressure of my concern for all the churches. Who is weak, and I do not feel weak? Who is led into sin, and I do not inwardly burn?
>
> If I must boast, I will boast of the things that show my weakness. The God and Father of the Lord Jesus, who is to be praised forever, knows that I am not lying. In Damascus the governor under King Aretas had the city of the Damascenes guarded in order to arrest me. But I was lowered in a basket from a window in the wall and slipped through his hands" (2 Cor. 11:23-33).

We see Paul face all kinds of adversity and dangers, both external and internal. This adversity brought many losses: comfort, security, safety, sleep, food, home, health, peace, and physical and mental rest. However, this was a deeply fruitful and successful life. Paul advanced the Gospel, planted churches, wrote the epistles—which are part of the Holy Bible—and turned the world upside down.

The result was that he succeeded in his calling and mission, not only despite opposition and hardships, but because of them. The adversity just made him stronger in the Lord, more mature, braver, more resolute, and more resilient. God's presence was always with him to protect and deliver him. Also, the Holy Spirit gave him many revelations and visions of God and his kingdom, together with supernatural wisdom and understanding. That's why Paul chose to boast about his hardships and weaknesses. He didn't see them as obstacles, but as opportunities to grow and experience God's grace and power—what a powerful example to follow.

Declarations

- Adversity trains my faith muscles and helps me grow spiritually, become mature, and be able to carry heavier loads without breaking.
- Adversity is part of God's special preparation and training for his kingdom.
- God loves me and he wants to bless me in and through adversity.
- God will infuse me with strength and will help me in every situation.
- Unmet expectations are designed to propel me closer to God, to enable me "to grasp how wide and long and high and deep is the love of Christ" (Eph. 3:18).

Losses and Gains

Losses When I Face Adversity
1. The loss of comfort and ease
2. The loss of the sense of control (life, circumstances, people, outcomes)
3. The loss of the sense of security, safety, and protection
4. The loss of happiness
5. The loss of fulfilled desires and plans

Gains When I Draw Near to God
1. The gain of personal transformation in the image of Christ
2. The gain of spiritual growth and maturity
3. The gain of increased capacity to receive God's unconditional joy
4. The gain of learning to be content in all circumstances
5. The gain of learning to live by faith and not by sight
6. The gain of learning to surrender oneself, people, and circumstances continually to God
7. The gain of accepting my weaknesses unconditionally
8. The gain of experiencing God's strength and the victory of Christ in overcoming adversity
9. The gain of becoming stronger and more resilient
10. The gain of learning to follow God's plan and leading
11. The gain of learning to resist temptation
12. The gain of learning patience, humility, and long-suffering
13. The gain of fresh revelations, supernatural wisdom, and understanding
14. The gain of preparation for service and ministry

Reflection Questions

1. What is the biggest adversity you have overcome? What were your greatest losses and greatest gains?
2. What kind of adversity are you facing now?

Meditation Verses

"We are hard pressed on every side, but not crushed; perplexed, but not in despair; persecuted, but not abandoned; struck down, but not destroyed" (2 Cor. 4:8-9).

"I know what it is to be in need, and I know what it is to have plenty. I have learned the secret of being content in any and every situation, whether well fed or hungry, whether living in plenty or in want. I can do all this through him who gives me strength" (Phil. 4:12-13).

"And the God of all grace, who called you to his eternal glory in Christ, after you have suffered a little while, will himself restore you and make you strong, firm and steadfast" (1 Pet. 5:10).

"Consider it pure joy, my brothers and sisters, whenever you face trials of many kinds, because you know that the testing of your faith produces perseverance. Let perseverance finish its work so that you may be mature and complete, not lacking anything" (Jas. 1:2-4).

"And we know that in all things God works for the good of those who love him, who have been called according to his purpose" (Rom. 8:28).

"The righteous person may have many troubles, but the LORD delivers him from them all" (Ps. 34:19).

Hadassah Treu

Prayer

Dear Lord,

You know the hardships and adversity I am going through now. I choose to submit to your process of preparation and refining. I am deciding to consider my trials pure joy because the testing of my faith will produce perseverance, maturity, and spiritual growth.

Please, give me the strength to overcome and let me experience the victory of Christ in my circumstances and internal struggles. Make me strong, firm, and steadfast, and deliver me from all my troubles.

Lord, I surrender all my losses to you. Please bless me with eternal gains. Increase my capacity to receive your unconditional joy and peace, and teach me how to be content in all circumstances.

I submit my desires, plans, and expectations to you, too. Help me follow your leading and plan for my life.

In Jesus' name. Amen.

2
The Gifts Hidden in Sadness

I left my coffee where I met a friend and trudged home in the golden summer evening. My heart felt heavy, pierced by a sharp pain. Tears welled in my eyes. I felt the urge to cry. And, my thoughts were in unison with my body. I just thought to myself how sad I was to be alone this summer evening, going back to my empty home, where nobody waited for me. I imagined how wonderful it would have been if my husband were alive. Then, we would be together, walking, perhaps having dinner, and enjoying a wonderful evening. I was stretching the hands of my heart to take hold of him and lock him in my embrace, but my hands remained empty. The sadness enveloped me like a dark, heavy cloud pressing with heaviness on my chest, causing sighs and tears.

    I felt similar when I struggled with infertility. I was down most of the days, my thoughts were gloomy, and I struggled with hopelessness. The unfulfilled desire to become a mother was a constant source of sadness in my life for years. However, God's presence was also with me as a source of joy, delight, hope, and comfort.

    It is not funny being sad. So many things can make us sad—both small and big. Sometimes we experience sadness just for a moment; sometimes it is our prevailing mood for days or months, easily turning to depression. But what exactly is sadness? And why do we get sad?

According to The Merriam-Webster Dictionary, sadness is "affected by or expressive of grief or unhappiness (downcast). It is also causing or associated with grief or unhappiness (depressing)."[3] Wikipedia defines sadness as:

> "an emotional pain associated with or characterized by feelings of disadvantage, loss, despair, grief, helplessness, disappointment, and sorrow. An individual experiencing sadness may become quiet or lethargic and withdraw from others. An example of severe sadness is depression, a mood that can be brought on by major depressive disorder or persistent depressive disorder. Crying can be an indication of sadness. Sadness is one of the six basic emotions described by Paul Ekman, along with happiness, anger, surprise, fear, and disgust."[4]

In the Bible, there are several Greek words to describe sadness. The first is *penthos*, meaning mourning, sorrow, sadness, and grief. The second is *katepheia* meaning dejection, downcast in look; demureness, i.e. (by implication) sadness and heaviness. The third one is *lupeo* meaning to distress, to grieve, and to experience deep emotional pain and sorrow. The next word is *lupe*—the pain of body or mind, grief, sorrow, and heaviness. The last word is *mochthos* meaning toil, hardship, painfulness, travail, sadness.[5]

There are also different Hebrew words used for sadness, such as *roa* meaning badness, evil, ugliness, and rottenness. There is also the word *astab*, used in Genesis 6:6 to show the emotion God felt and his deep disappointment with humanity. *Astab* means to suffer pain, grief hurt, and emotional torment.[6]

The Loss of Joy and the Greater Joy

When we are sad, the first things we lose are our feelings of

---

[3] https://www.merriam-webster.com/dictionary/sad
[4] https://en.wikipedia.org/wiki/Sadness
[5] https://biblehub.com/topical/s/sadness.htm
[6] https://www.chaimbentorah.com/2019/05/hebrew-word-study-sadness/

joy, happiness, and contentment based on favorable circumstances. It is good to feel joy and happiness based on our circumstances, but the problem is that "each day has enough trouble of its own" (Matt. 6:34). What do we do when we lose this conditional joy and is it possible to experience another kind of joy even in our sadness and sorrow?

Yes, there is a greater, higher joy, which is a constant, deep state of the soul. This condition is the product of intimacy and communion with God. That is the joy of our transformation.

The greater joy is the joy of knowing and practicing the reality of the living God and his unconditional love and acceptance. It is the joy of appeasement of the soul, of satisfying its deepest needs. And, they are the needs for unconditional love, acceptance, value, purpose, significance, security, and safety. This is how David describes this joy, "You have put more joy in my heart than they have when their grain and wine abound. In peace, I will both lie down and sleep; for you alone, oh Lord, make me dwell in safety" (Ps. 4:7-8 ESV).

The greater joy is not born and does not depend on gains and achievements. Its birthplace is in our acceptance of God's life and nature through faith in the Lord Jesus Christ. This is the process of restoration of our souls, of deliverance, and healing the broken hearts. This process involves the opening of the eyes and gaining wholeness and integrity. It is the joy of filling the void in the soul with the living waters from the true source.

Our greater joy rests on the simple but revolutionary truth that God is always with us and that he works tirelessly in and for us. This is the understanding and the practical experience of the fact that we can call upon the Almighty God at any time. There is confidence in that he hears and answers us so we can enjoy and rejoice in him every minute. The joy of walking with God is the joy of experiencing him not only as the lover of our souls but also as our shaper. It is the God who gives our souls a new form and image and brings them into a state of prosperity and satisfaction.

I love the prayer of Habakkuk because it is about finding joy in a season of sadness and suffering:

> "Though the fig tree does not bud and there are no grapes on the vines, though the olive crop fails and the fields produce no food, though there are no sheep in the pen and no cattle in the stalls, yet I will rejoice in the Lord, I will be joyful in God my Savior. The Sovereign Lord is my strength; he makes my feet like the feet of a deer; he enables me to tread on the heights" (Hab. 3:17-19).

We can make this powerful prayer our personal prayer in a season of sadness: even though I am stricken with sadness and sorrow, even though I am afflicted, even though I have lost my loved one, even though I have lost my job, I will yet rejoice in the Lord: even though I experience health problems, even though I live in uncertain times, I will yet be joyful in my Savior. I will rejoice in his love, his character, his promises, and his presence.

The Three Levels of Hope

The next thing we may lose in our sadness is our hope. It is very easy to start struggling with hopelessness when we are sad and depressed. Even though we may lose our temporary hope, in Christ, we still have our constant, personified hope.

Let's take a look at these three levels of hope:

- The hopes for our earthly life and life circumstances
- The deeper hopes for our spiritual well-being and soul wholeness
- The deepest hopes and longings for heaven on earth

Regarding our hopes for our life circumstances, we need to remember that God always provides for our immediate needs as the psalmist declares, "The Lord is my shepherd, I lack nothing" (Ps. 23:1).

Even when our lives don't turn out as we want and expect them to, we still have God's promise to meet our deeper hopes and longings. In Christ, God provides the ultimate solution to our spiritual problems. In him, we have constant provision for our souls and spirits. Through him, we receive spiritual restoration and have constant access to the throne of grace. He is the good shepherd and nothing can snatch us from his hand.

The believer's life on earth is not easy. We will be tempted, tested, and will experience sadness, suffering, and loss. In such a time of deep suffering, we need a hope that doesn't shake, one that is not tethered to visible, shaky things. We need the assurance that God will satisfy our deepest longings.

Our hearts cry to God with the psalmist, "Take my side as you promised; I'll live then for sure. Don't disappoint all my grand hopes" (Ps. 119:116 MSG).

No, God will not disappoint our grand hopes: the hopes for the redemption of our bodies and heaven on earth, and the hopes for our eternal future. It is safe for us to anchor our greatest hope to God's irrevocable promise of the renewal of all things; the grand restoration, a new heaven, and a new earth (Isa. 65:17-25, Rev. 21, Matt. 19:28-30).

The Greatest Possible Comfort

When we are sad, we also have the awesome opportunity to experience God's comfort and compassion firsthand. There is nothing comparable to God's comfort. But what is comfort? Comfort often means providing strength, hope, and help. Yes, we need strength to endure the pain. We also need hope to keep going and trust that we will see good in our lives. And, we need help. It could be a practical kind of help to solve an overwhelming problem, help to see things from another perspective, or help to start healing.

The most important gain in our sadness is to experience that the Lord is Jehovah-Shammah—the Lord is there (Ezek. 48:35)—our comforter and helper.

The Lord showed up at the beginning of the book of Ezekiel in the least likely place the Jews expected him—in the place of their captivity and exile—he showed up in Babylon! We need to keep in mind that the Jews had a very strict religious system and followed the Law. They expected the Lord's presence to appear in his temple, but definitely not in Babylon.

Not only did the Lord appear in Babylon, but he also appeared to the prophet Ezekiel in a majestic, glorious, breathtaking vision that simply blew Ezekiel away. Can you imagine seeing God in his glory, majesty, and beauty, seated on his throne carried by the four living creatures (Ezek. 1:22-28)?

Then at the end of the book, when describing the future city and dwelling of his people, the Lord revealed his constant presence and care with the name Jehovah Shammah, meaning "the Lord is there" (Ezek. 48:35).

What does this mean for us in our sadness and suffering?

It means that the Lord is there, always present and intimately involved in our earthly lives, while preparing us for eternity with him. We can see the marks of him being there in our preservation, endurance, and overcoming adversity.

The fact that the Lord is there is the greatest possible comfort! He is there in the ruins, in the pain, in the garbage, in the suffering, in the darkness, and in the hopelessness. He not only knows, he also feels our pain. The Lord is there—knowing, feeling, holding, comforting, and working. Jesus is our Emmanuel (God with us) and this truth is the greatest possible comfort in every painful circumstance that causes us sadness.

The Story of Jeremiah

Let's take a look at a couple of biblical examples showing us how God comes closer in our sadness and comforts and transforms us.

One of the best examples is the prophet Jeremiah. He is the author of two books in the Bible: Jeremiah and Lamentations.

God chose Jeremiah before birth to be a prophet of the nation of Judah (Jer. 1:4–50). He spoke the words of the Lord during the reigns of Kings Josiah (2 Chron. 36:1), Jehoiakim (2 Chron. 36:5), and Zedekiah (2 Kings 24:18–19). Jeremiah grieved over the wickedness of his people and the impending judgment the nation's sins had provoked. His warnings went mostly unheeded, and he responded to Judah's rebellion with tears of mourning (Jer. 13:17). Jeremiah has been called "the weeping prophet" because of the often gloomy nature of his message and the grief he expressed for his people.

Here is how Jeremiah expresses his sadness in the Book of Lamentations, "My eyes fail from weeping, I am in torment within; my heart is poured out on the ground because my people are destroyed, because children and infants faint in the streets of the city" (Lam. 2:11).

Here we see an example of extreme sadness and sorrow. Like the book of Job, Lamentations pictures a man of God puzzling over the results of evil and suffering in the world. But at the heart of this book, at the center of this lament over the effects of sin in the world, sit a few verses devoted to hope in the Lord. This statement of faith, that stands strong amid the surrounding darkness, shines as a beacon to all those suffering under the consequences of their sin and disobedience.

In his sadness, Jeremiah has the awesome opportunity to be supported by the God of all comfort and compassion. Remembering who God is and his compassionate nature changed Jeremiah's outlook and he could express hope and make peace with the situation.

Here are his hope-filled words:

> "I remember my affliction and my wandering, the bitterness and the gall. I well remember them, and my soul is downcast within me. Yet this I call to mind and therefore I have hope: Because of the Lord's great love we are not consumed, for his compassions never fail. They are new every morning; great is your faithfulness. I say to myself, 'The Lord is my portion; therefore I will wait for

him.' The Lord is good to those whose hope is in him, to the one who seeks him; it is good to wait quietly for the salvation of the Lord" (Lam. 3:19-26).

Jeremiah's sadness opened the way for him to experience God as his ultimate source of comfort. This is the greatest gift and blessing. Here is what the prophet said, "God, you are my comfort when I am very sad and when I am afraid" (Jer. 8:18 NCV).

As in the case of Jeremiah, our sadness enables us to draw near to the Lord and also prompts the Lord to draw near to us. The sadness is an open door to experience God as our all-encompassing comfort, joy, peace, and hope. Experiencing God's compassion helps us develop self-compassion and acceptance instead of wallowing in self-pity. Lastly, sadness drives us to develop a closer relationship with God and to cultivate friendship and intimacy with him.

The Prophet Elijah's Extreme Sadness

There is another example of extreme sadness and how God takes care of the suffering person and helps change his perspective. This is the story of the prophet Elijah after his greatest victory over Baal and his prophets. Elijah had a big show-down with the prophets of Baal on Mount Carmel. After he prayed to God, fire came down from heaven and consumed the sacrifice and the stones of the altar. Then, Elijah had all the prophets of Baal killed. This was an enormous victory, defending the name of the living God. However, when this happened, Queen Jezebel said she would kill Elijah, so in fear, he left his servant behind and ran into the wilderness where he sat under a broom tree and prayed he would die (1 Kings 19:4).

How did God treat Elijah in his sadness and depression? He treated him with the utmost tenderness, giving him new perspective, hope, encouragement, and mission. First, he sent an angel to bring him food and drink to sustain him physically. Then, the Lord himself appeared to Elijah (1 Kings 19:9-18).

Isn't this amazing? Our sadness and suffering prompt the Lord not only to send angels to sustain us, but also to give us a fresh revelation of himself providing spiritual nourishment and blessing. The Lord chose to reveal his presence to Elijah in one of the tenderest ways: as a gentle whisper, that was a balm to Elijah's weary soul. The Lord didn't choose to reveal his presence as the powerful forces of wind, earthquake, and fire. No, he chose the gentle whisper to comfort and encourage Elijah. The Lord communicated with Elijah, asking him questions, so Elijah could express his pain and the reason behind it. The Lord not only comforted Elijah, but he also addressed Elijah's complaint. He revealed new information that assured Elijah he was not alone and gave him a new purpose and mission. The Lord gave Elijah a reason to live at the lowest point of his sadness and depression.

We can take heart from this example. Even when our sadness and depression are overwhelming and difficult to bear, it is still an open door to experience the most tender aspects of God's character. We become recipients of his provision for our physical, emotional, and spiritual needs, as shown in Elijah's story.

Declarations

- Even though I am stricken with sadness and sorrow, even though I am afflicted, I will rejoice in the Lord. I will rejoice in his love, in his character, in his promises, and in his presence.
- In my sorrow, I have access to a greater, higher joy based on the fact that God is always with me and he works tirelessly in me, through me, and for me.
- My sorrow opens the door to experience God as the God of all comfort and compassion.

- Even if I may lose my temporary hope, I still have my constant, personified hope in Christ.
- In my sadness, the Lord is there—knowing, feeling, holding, comforting, and working.

Losses and Gains

Losses When I Face Sadness
1. The loss of joy and happiness
2. The loss of hope
3. The loss of satisfaction and contentment
4. The loss of a treasured thing (a person, relationship, etc.)

Gains When I Draw Near to God
1. The gain of an increased capacity to receive God's comfort and to know him as the God of all comfort
2. The gain of increased capacity to receive God's mercy and compassion
3. The gain of increased capacity to receive God's unconditional joy and peace
4. The gain of an opportunity to become a comforter and comfort others with the comfort we have received from God
5. The gain of learning to have self-compassion and acceptance
6. The gain of learning to have hope in all circumstances
7. The gain of developing a positive, hopeful outlook in circumstances causing sadness
8. The gain of fresh revelations and supernatural wisdom and understanding
9. The gain of cultivating friendship and intimacy with God
10. The gain of spiritual growth and maturity
11. The gain of personal transformation in the image of Christ

Reflection Questions

1. What makes you sad at the moment? What is the reason for your sadness?
2. What is the greatest gain for you when you experience sadness?

Meditation Verses

"Praise be to the God and Father of our Lord Jesus Christ, the Father of compassion and the God of all comfort, who comforts us in all our troubles, so that we can comfort those in any trouble with the comfort we ourselves receive from God" (2 Cor. 1:3-4).

"For his anger lasts only a moment, but his favor lasts a lifetime; weeping may stay for the night, but rejoicing comes in the morning" (Ps. 30:5).

"The Lord is close to the brokenhearted and saves those who are crushed in spirit" (Ps. 34:18).

"All my longings lie open before you, Lord; my sighing is not hidden from you" (Ps. 38:9).

"He will wipe every tear from their eyes. There will be no more death or mourning or crying or pain, for the old order of things has passed away" (Rev. 21:4).

"Godly sorrow brings repentance that leads to salvation and leaves no regret, but worldly sorrow brings death" (2 Cor. 7:10).

Hadassah Treu

Prayer

Dear Lord,

I struggle with sadness and sorrow. You know my losses and the reasons behind my sadness. Lord, please come and comfort me. Let me know you as the God of all comfort and the Father of all mercy and compassion. Please bring strength, encouragement, and help into my life.

Lord, let this sadness become an open door to experience your unconditional joy and peace that doesn't depend on my circumstances and my feelings. Instill in me fresh hope, oh Lord, and don't disappoint my grand hopes.

Set me free from self-pity and victim mentality and help me learn self-compassion and acceptance.

Lord, give me a fresh revelation of your presence and love. Wrap me in your arms and make me a comforter and encourager so I can love others well and help them in their sadness. I surrender my sadness to you.

In Jesus' name. Amen.

3

The Gifts Hidden in Anxiety

It is difficult to accurately describe how a panic attack feels. It starts usually without a warning, completely out of the blue. I am relaxed in one moment and then in the next second my world is turning inside out and I am entering another reality in which I am drowning—mighty, terrifying, dark waves engulf me. I struggle to breathe and to come out.

My body stands at the epicenter of an earthquake, and every cell of mine is shaking and disintegrating. It is as if the core of my being is breaking, and the shock waves are spreading across every muscle in my body.

Something dangerous with the power to kill overcomes me. I fear I am dying because of the complete loss of control over my reactions. My heart beats with furious speed. Cold sweat streams from every pore of my skin, and my limbs tremble convulsively. I am sinking into a black abyss, and I can't get out. The outside world recedes.

It is an agony, a completely out-of-control situation, the purest terror. One can only endure the agony and cry out with some remainder of consciousness for the earthquake to stop, and the raging sea to calm down.

In 2014, they diagnosed me with general anxiety disorder and panic attacks. This was the year when I found out that I was infertile and would never become a mother in a normal way. I could not understand how God allowed that situation: not only my infertility, but also the anxiety disorder. It seemed the more I prayed and searched for him, the more my situation got worse.

Now, with the distance of time, I can see and appreciate all the beautiful fruits that came out of my struggle with anxiety and panic attacks. It was worth enduring this suffering for a short time so I could have all blessings of eternal value after that. This was God's way of healing me, making me whole, and bringing me into a deeper surrender.

It was worth enduring the temporary losses that came wrapped up in the anxiety-fears-panic attacks package. The scariest traumatic loss when struggling with anxiety is the loss of our sense of control. This leads to losing our sense of security, safety, and protection. Anxiety may invade our lives when we lose relationships or loved ones, or when a desired outcome doesn't come.

Anxiety and the Fear of the Lord

The primary cause of anxiety is our desire to control things, people, and circumstances. Control is our path to security and safety, which is a basic need for all human beings. We often define safety as the absence of events and people that can pose some kind of threat to our comfort and way of life. This pushes us into the behavior of preventing unwanted events or results, on one hand, and securing a desired result on the other. However, God's will and desire are to deliver us from all our fears from which anxiety grows. He wants to build and strengthen us in the fear of the Lord and into faith and trust in him.

Growth in the fear of the Lord and learning to walk by faith and not by sight are among the first and most precious benefits buried in our struggle with anxiety. The fear of the Lord is the healthiest, as it prompts us to run away from evil and sinful attitudes and deeds (Prov. 8:13). It acts as the most powerful antidote and therapy against all other fears and worries. God calls the fear of him "the beginning of wisdom" (Prov. 9:10) and "a fountain of life," as in adding length to our life (Prov. 14:27).

The fear of the Lord is the attitude of awe and reverence to God as the only almighty and sovereign God, creator, and master of creation. It is an attitude that acknowledges God as the only one who has the supreme authority over everything and everyone, including life and death. We fear the Lord when we believe he is the one he says he is and the one who has the last word, the judge of the living and the dead.

Learning to live in the light of God's sovereignty is another precious gift when we battle anxiety and fear. Ezekiel chapter one contains a vivid description of a vision of God's glory and sovereignty, represented by the four living creatures carrying the throne of God:

> "Above the vault over their heads was what looked like a throne of lapis lazuli, and high above on the throne was a figure like that of a man. I saw that from what appeared to be his waist up he looked like glowing metal, as if full of fire, and that from there down he looked like fire; and brilliant light surrounded him. Like the appearance of a rainbow in the clouds on a rainy day, so was the radiance around him.
>
> This was the appearance of the likeness of the glory of the Lord. When I saw it, I fell facedown, and I heard the voice of one speaking" (Ezek. 1:26-28).

The Need to Surrender and the Gift of God's Peace

Anxiety contains another powerful gift if we choose to unwrap it. This is the possibility of giving up our peace and embracing God's peace instead. There are two kinds of peace. The first is our kind of peace—meaning we are relaxed and confident when things go our way, and according to our expectations, wishes, and plans. Naturally, this peace is disturbed by every single thing or problem that does not fit in our scenarios. Then, we usually react by trying to keep our little worlds under control. The more we try, the more our anxiety rises.

Then there is this wonderful gift—God's peace. It is available for every believer through the Holy Spirit. This is a supernatural peace: the product of our acknowledgment of the loving presence of God. This is peace of mind rooted in the confidence that God loves us, that he is always with us, and that he is working for our best interests. And, that he is in control because only he has the power and the wisdom to run the show.

The path to go from our shaky kind of peace to God's peace is called surrender. We consciously, by faith, choose to release control; we make known our prayers and concerns to God with thanksgiving and by submitting situations and people to his control. Here are God's instructions on how to do this, "Do not be anxious about anything, but in every situation, by prayer and petition, with thanksgiving, present your requests to God. And the peace of God, which transcends all understanding, will guard your hearts and your minds in Christ Jesus" (Phil. 4:6-7).

Unconditional surrender to God is not merely a promise to obey him no matter what our usual operating mode is. No, it is a relinquishing of one's entire self—including our inabilities and perceived abilities into his hands—that he might do whatever is necessary to glorify Christ in and through us.

Giving God the freedom to do as he sees fit with us is the safest choice we can make for one simple reason: he is our creator, and the one loving us completely and unconditionally with eternal love. He has only good in mind for the people who belong to him. God has done and always does what is best for us, from an eternal perspective, and what is best for his glory.

During my struggle with anxiety and panic attacks, I had to embrace the practice of surrender as a continual process. I needed to accept that God would continue to bring me into situations that would call for surrender.

God's constant call to surrender is his way and therapy to set us free from any form of repressed anger, resentment, bitterness, and disappointment. Holding on to control and trying to keep things together is the path to panic and anxiety disorder. God's path to breaking free is learning to surrender and trust him as the one who runs the show and as the controller and manager of all things. This is his recipe for peace, confidence, and rest. Everything else is just temporary relief from symptoms, but not a real cure.

Anxiety as an Opportunity to Change Our Fearful Thinking

When we choose to see the anxiety, fears, and panic attacks as instruments in the hand of God to establish us in our true selves and the image of Christ, they can become a blessed opportunity and invitation to transform our minds and thought patterns, and to live a life in greater freedom and peace.

Everything that happens to us is right in its place, is best for us, is at the right moment, and is done in the best way for us to grow. The loving hand of God guides everything. God teaches us not to resist His ways and not to fight against our true selves. Through the panic attacks and anxiety disorder, God gives us the strength to remain completely naked and exposed to ourselves and him, without the cover-ups of our defense mechanisms. This is an open invitation to accept our weaknesses unconditionally and surrender to God without reservation.

Fear and anxiety have many faces, levels, and nuances—the panic attack is just one of these. There is an interesting illustration called the scale of fear. This is a scale with levels from ten to zero, where specific physical manifestations and symptoms correspond to each level of fear and anxiety. For example, for levels ten to six, the person cannot exercise volitional control over the physical manifestations of fear and panic. Levels five to one are characterized by general anxiety: starting with the beginning of a panic attack and then followed by three more levels of anxiety with different intensities of expressions, the weakest form being butterflies in the stomach. Level zero is the one of complete relaxation.

The movement from ten to zero is a journey in which, at each stage, God blesses us with victory, new strength, and understanding. He gives us a roadmap of healing and freedom. On my journey, I have celebrated many victories. I learned to face and overcome the panic attacks, the fear of panic attacks, the fear of the symptoms, and the state of expecting the next panic attack.

The even greater victory was to identify and eliminate thought patterns and behaviors that could trigger panic attacks and to allow the Holy Spirit to transform my fearful thinking into courageous and faith-filled thinking. I gained the freedom to react in the way I feel, and not the way I thought I needed to please others. I learned to live in agreement with my true self, giving myself grace and compassion.

In my struggles, God also gave me the courage to address and overcome the fear of the future and the fear of the unknown. He taught me how to cultivate hope and the joyful expectation that the future would bring me good things—my weapon against the fear of the future. Finally, I was holding the weapon of trust, enabling me to be ready to take risks and welcome the new things that I don't have control over, with the confidence that God is the controller of it all.

This was my tailor-made weapon against the fear of the unknown.

Biblical Strategies to Deal with Anxiety and Fears

Last but not least, I learned and practiced biblical strategies to deal with anxiety and fear. Remembering and forgetting are two powerful strategies that can transform our anxiety into fruitful soil for many blessings.

We are called to remember God and meditate on his word daily. Psalm 105 is a beautiful invitation and prompt to acknowledge God's presence and do life with him with a thankful heart.

Remembering God helps us to redirect our attention from the negative thought patterns that cause anxiety and worry and shift it to the rock, to our centre of stability. God's Word instructs us to remember his love, his faithfulness, his words and promises, and his deeds daily.

We do this by engaging in prayer and praise, by calling upon his name, and by reflecting and talking about what he has done for us in the past. We remember God by boasting his name, by singing, and by choosing to rejoice despite the circumstances. God invites us to a conscious choice to search and find our joy, shelter, and peace in him.

He is also a God who remembers—his covenant, his promises, all our sorrows, all our tears, all our deepest desires, and all our needs. He is a God who remembers us every day and chooses, through Christ, to forget our sins and transgressions.

We are to remember, but we are also to forget. It is our choice of what to remember and what to forget that moves us from a place of losses to a place of gains and blessings. What do we need to forget?

In the first place, these are our sins and the sins of others. There is no condemnation in Christ and God has called us to a lifestyle of forgiveness and soft hearts free from resentment, bitterness, and malice (Rom. 8:1). We are to forget the offenses and disappointments and learn to be humble. This means to live unoffended by submitting our rights to God and asking for healing for our wounds.

The second thing to forget is the past. God urges us to let go of the past and not dwell there. Instead, He invites us to see the new things he is doing every day (Isa. 43:18-19). In the description of the four living creatures that are carriers of God's glory, the prophet Ezekiel adds a very important detail; these creatures follow the Spirit of God and move only forward, without turning back (Ezek. 1:12, 10:11). This is our direction, too. Let's stop putting more energy into the "why" question. Instead, let's focus on new questions and issues, on the new things God is doing and showing us today.

The third thing to forget is the temporary things that do not matter for eternity. We need discernment and wisdom from God about this and the grace to choose rightly and invest ourselves in things that matter (Col. 3:1-2).

Declarations

- I give God the freedom to do as he sees fit with me because this is the safest choice I can make.
- God has only my good in mind because I belong to him. God has done and always does what is best for me (from an eternal perspective) and what is best for his glory.
- Everything that happens to me is right in its place, is best for me, is at the right moment, and is done in the best way for me to grow. Everything is guided by the loving hand of God.
- I choose not to resist God's ways and not to fight against my true self.
-

Losses and Gains

Losses When I Face Anxiety
1. The loss of self-control
2. The loss of the sense of control (over my life, over circumstances, people, outcomes)
3. The loss of the sense of security, safety, and protection
4. The loss of a desired outcome
5. The loss of peace

Gains When I Draw Near to God
1. The gain of personal transformation in the image of Christ
2. The gain of self-discovery

3. The gain of growth in the fear of the Lord
4. The gain of increased capacity to receive God's peace
5. The gain of learning to live by faith and not by sight
6. The gain of learning to surrender oneself, people, and circumstances continually to God
7. The gain of experiencing God's sovereignty
8. The gain of accepting my weaknesses unconditionally
9. The gain of healing and freedom from coping mechanisms
10. The gain of freedom from the fear of the future
11. The gain of freedom from the fear of the unknown
12. The gain of better and healthier relationships with myself and others

Reflection Questions

1. What is your biggest fear?
2. In which areas do you fear losing control? Why?
3. What is your greatest loss when struggling with anxiety?

Meditation Verses

"You will keep in perfect peace those whose minds are steadfast, because they trust in you" (Isa. 26:3).

"Do not be anxious about anything, but in every situation, by prayer and petition, with thanksgiving, present your requests to God. And the peace of God, which transcends all understanding, will guard your hearts and your minds in Christ Jesus" (Phil. 4:6-7).

"Even though I walk through the darkest valley, I will fear no evil, for you are with me; your rod and your staff, they comfort me" (Ps. 23:4).

"Surely your goodness and love will follow me all the days of my life, and I will dwell in the house of the LORD forever" (Ps. 23:6).

"But now, this is what the LORD says—he who created you, Jacob, he who formed you, Israel: Do not fear, for I have redeemed you; I have summoned you by name; you are mine. When you pass through the waters, I will be with you; and when you pass through the rivers, they will not sweep over you. When you walk through the fire, you will not be burned; the flames will not set you ablaze" (Isa. 43: 1-2).

Prayer

Dear Lord,
    My anxious thoughts are tormenting me. I need your peace. You have promised peace to the ones who love your Law. I love your Word, Lord, and I have hidden it in my heart. With you on my side, I will not stumble.

    Help me focus my thoughts on you and surrender everything and everyone that causes me to worry. I choose not to be anxious and am bringing all my problems and concerns to you, now. I leave them in your loving and capable hands. Thank you for your provision, Lord. Thank you for your constant care.

    Thank you for listening to my prayers and requests, and for answering them. Thank you for giving me your peace, that I may have it right here, right now, transcending all understanding, and guarding my heart and mind in Christ Jesus.

    Jesus, you are my peace. Amen.

4

The Gifts Hidden in Rejection

This was just one of many nights when I was lying in bed awake, tears streaming down my face. I heard the breathing of my husband, peacefully sleeping, not aware of my pain. It's not supposed to be this way, I thought.

I wanted to have children but felt that we were on different pages, far away from each other. Month after month, the alienation deepened. I felt alone, abandoned, and rejected as a wife and a woman. Bitterness, anger, and resentment filled my heart. Quarrels or cold silence ruled our days. Our marriage was dying, and I was dying on the inside by the poison of rejection. Continuous rejection of my strongest desire made me ill. It disturbed my body functions on multiple levels, even to the extent of developing antibodies produced by my thyroid gland. My body was turning against me.

I dragged myself day by day as a wounded animal, begging and hoping to feel loved again, accepted, and cherished. Like a hungry beggar, I was searching and collecting every bread crumble of attention, affection, and every promise for a change. But I also turned to God and poured out my heart to him, praying for a restoration of my marriage and a change in my husband. Interestingly, God was much more concerned with healing and restoring my heart first.

In my anguish of feeling like a rejected and abandoned woman, God spoke to me through Isaiah 54. Through the words of the prophet, God helped me shift my focus from my husband as a satisfier of my needs towards God. The words of Isaiah gave me a passionate vision of God as my first love, best friend, the ultimate satisfaction, and the source of my blessings.

It was revolutionary and unseemly to see God as my husband, but it fulfilled my need for unconditional love and acceptance. To accept and respond to this intimate invitation was God's way of helping me deal with my husband's rejection. This freed me to love him back without the burden of placing my expectations on him.

Besides adding a new aspect and deepening my relationship with God, this painful rejection taught me another thing about love, too. When we experience and believe in God's love, it is possible by the power of the Holy Spirit to love the people who have rejected us despite our pain. Our suffering and hurt are not in vain when they help us grow our own outpouring of love. Has a person who is supposed to love and respect you, also rejected you?

The Sting of Rejection

Rejection is a form of exclusion, non-acceptance, dismissal, abandonment, and forsaking. Rejection is "the act of refusing to accept, use, or believe someone or something but also the act of not giving someone the love and attention they want and expect."[7] Merriam-Webster Dictionary defines rejection as the refusal "to accept, consider, submit to, take for some purpose, or use; to refuse to hear, receive, or admit, and to refuse as a lover or spouse.'"[8]

Rejection equals a small death. A part of us is dying when we are rejected. We are split internally and our souls scream and want to withdraw. We struggle with myriads of internal sensations and

---

[7] https://dictionary.cambridge.org/dictionary/english/rejection
[8] https://www.merriam-webster.com/dictionary/reject

responses like shock and disbelief, questioning our beliefs and relationships, and doubting our self-worth.

Rejection is truly one of the most painful human experiences. It cuts to the core of our beings and projects powerful and heart-shattering messages like:

> *You are not enough.*
> *Your work is not good enough.*
> *You are not loved.*
> *You don't deserve it.*
> *You don't belong.*
> *You are worthless.*
> *You will never measure up.*

These harmful messages can damage our identity and relationships with God, ourselves, and others if we believe and internalize them. We can experience rejection on many levels—we can be rejected as persons in a relationship, or in a group and community. Also, people can reject our work, projects, ideas, or ministry. This can cause deep wounds too, especially when we identify ourselves with our work.

I will never forget my first submission and first rejection as a new writer. It took months to write my first manuscript, a lot of hard work and emotional turmoil. I was overconfident and convinced that since I had invested time and effort, and it was clearly God's calling, it would work. I couldn't imagine that my work could get rejected. When I received the publisher's negative response, it hit me like a bomb. My legs were suddenly shaking, and I needed to sit down. Blood was rushing through my veins and my face got red and hot. My chest tightened and my insides were quivering.

The rejection blasted my carefully constructed palace of expectations and plans for how my writing career would develop. I needed time and God's power to pick up and clear the debris of wrong assumptions, expectations, and attitudes.

Rejection's Transformational Potential

It turned out that this first rejection and the many more to follow were God's gifts to transform me. In the first place, I needed to separate myself from my work. My value as a person is not dependent on my accomplishments and success. God continued to love me before and after the rejection of my work. His love and grace never cease; I needed to learn to rest in the unconditional love of the Father and to learn to draw my value from my identity as a beloved child of God. It is so easy to fall away from God's grace and start living by rules. But the truth is, I am not my work, and neither are you your work.

Another important gain from the rejections I continue to receive in my work is that they test and train my perseverance and self-discipline. As frail humans, we prefer the shortcut or the easy way. We don't like delays, detours, and obstacles on the way. But this is not God's way. God's way is not always straightforward from A to B. It might involve zigzags, stops, circles, and redirections. Why is he making things difficult for us, as it seems?

One reason is to test our hearts and motivations and teach us to depend on him. This is part of our calling to walk by faith, not by sight. But another crucial reason, intended as a blessing and gift for us, is to develop perseverance, long-suffering, tenacity, and resilience. These are invaluable character traits and part of the fruit of the Spirit, a testimony of God's work and power in our lives.

Last but not least, very often rejection is God's tool of protection and redirection. Several years later, after my first rejection, I could gain an understanding that I was not ready for the publication process. It was premature and simply not the right time. God knew better. He was wise and loving enough to let me experience this rejection and redirect me on his path of growth. He knew my heart needed to mature.

The Losses of Rejection

The first loss is self-worth. This blow to our self-perception and awareness steals from our self-dignity and damages our identity. Our thoughts switch to a negative script telling us we are not loved because we are not lovable and we don't deserve love. Our true selves become blurred and go into hiding.

This leads to the next loss: the loss of self-confidence. When we doubt our self-worth, we naturally lose our confidence and the fear of people grows. We either want people's approval or fear their disapproval. We fall into people-pleasing tendencies to avoid being rejected again.

When our work, projects, and ideas get rejected, we often lose our motivation. We find it difficult to believe in the value and quality of our work and our motivation and passion diminish. Why continue doing something when people will reject it?

Rejection often leads to a loss of courage, too. The pain of rejection weakens our whole being and opens a door to fear and anxiety. As a result, we may find it difficult to move courageously forward and try new things and projects, or enter new relationships.

Finally, with rejection, we may lose a relationship with a person or with a group of people. Yes, rejection may put an end to a relationship, or at least the existing form of a relationship.

For example, the rejection I experienced in my marriage put an end to the way I perceived my husband and the vision I had for our relationship. I wished for myself a normal family with one or two children, but this dream was put to an end.

If rejection is so deadly, why would God allow it and why is it a gift? What are the hidden blessings in a rejection blow? To answer this question, let's turn to several stories of rejection in the Bible.

Hagar: Rejected as a Woman, Wife, and Mother

I love the story of Hagar in the Old Testament because this is the story of a used and rejected woman, just thrown away and disposed of when she is no longer of any use.

Isn't this the story of so many women nowadays?

We meet Hagar in Genesis 16 and 21. She is the slave of Sarah, Abraham's wife, who is barren. God made Abraham an awesome, mind-blowing promise: God would make him the father of God's chosen nation, and his descendants would be as numerous as the sand grains. (Gen. 12:1-3) But years and years passed by and nothing happened. So Sarah, still called Sarai at the time of these events, took matters into her own hands and used Hagar as a surrogate mother.

Hagar had no choice. She did what she was told to do, and she conceived. This changed the dynamic in the family and Sarah started mistreating Hagar. And what was Abraham doing? Nothing. He simply gave Sarah a green light to do whatever she wished with Hagar. So it is not a surprise that Hagar fled in the desert (Gen. 16:6). But there was a greater surprise waiting; an angel from the Lord appeared, gave her a personal promise and message from the Lord, and instructed her to go back home to her mistress.

Let's hold on here for a while. God sent an angel! This means God himself was present with Hagar in a powerful, manifested way. He came to this woman with his presence and brought encouragement, comfort, vision for the future, and a magnificent promise (Gen. 16:12). Hagar saw the angel and heard the words, but most importantly she heard love and acceptance behind the words and she trusted the message. She heard:

I see you. You are valuable to me.
I love you.
I accept you.
I have a plan for you.
I will take care of you.
You are not abandoned and rejected.
That's why you can go back.

Why can we be sure she heard and embraced this message?

Because she gave a name to the Lord right there, right then. She gave this name to the Lord who spoke to her: "You are the God who sees me," for she said, "I have now seen the one who sees me." (Gen 16:13). She felt seen and known by God, but she also saw him in a new light and experienced an intimate fellowship with him. God saw her, and she saw him.

How awesome is it that God sees us? Imagine this for a moment. God sees, understands, and loves every part of our beings. He sees our past, present, and future. God sees the hurt and all invisible wounds in our hearts. He sees the light and the darkness. And he stays; he does not reject. He sees our true selves, all parts coming together and his plan unfolding. Rejection is a powerful invitation and opportunity to open our eyes to see and love him as the one who sees us.

Once more, Hagar experienced rejection when Abraham and Sarah sent her away in the desert with her son Ishmael (Gen. 21:8-20). This time, it was a final rejection from Abraham's family, but God not only saved her life but the life of the boy in the desert. He also kept his promise to take care of him and make him a great nation.

The Rejected Prophet

The Bible is full of stories of God's servants, whose ministries the people widely rejected. Actually, it was the rule and not the exception. Nearly all Old Testament prophets were rejected because of their message, especially when the message was one of God's judgment and impending destruction. We also don't need to look further than Jesus, the very Son of God. The vast majority of the Jews, including the religious leaders at that time, rejected him and his message, leading to his death on the cross. This was, of course, all part of God's providential plan.

Let's again shift our focus to the prophet Jeremiah and learn from his story about the losses and gains of rejection. When God called Jeremiah to be a prophet, he warned him that people would reject him and his message.

Nevertheless, God himself would sustain and support him and give him the strength to carry on.

> "'Get yourself ready! Stand up and say to them whatever I command you. Do not be terrified by them, or I will terrify you before them. Today I have made you a fortified city, an iron pillar, and a bronze wall to stand against the whole land—against the kings of Judah, its officials, its priests, and the people of the land. They will fight against you but will not overcome you, for I am with you and will rescue you' declares the LORD" (Jer. 1:17-19).

This is such a powerful encouragement! We can glean two precious blessings the Lord has tucked in Jeremiah's experience of rejection. The first is the opportunity to be free from the fear of man and people-pleasing tendencies. Our people-pleasing tendencies can be a powerful stumbling block in serving the Lord and having wholeness and peace. Listen to the word of Paul: "Am I now trying to win the approval of human beings, or of God? Or am I trying to please people? If I were still trying to please people, I would not be a servant of Christ" (Gal.1:10).

The second powerful blessing and gain is to experience and know personally the Lord as our mighty defender, protector, and warrior. This is the blessing to know experientially that the Lord is enough. His presence with us is enough in every situation and what we need most. Against the backdrop of painful rejection, his indwelling and enveloping presence fortifies us internally and delivers us externally.

Besides, God himself takes care of our reputation with the promise to reward our faithful service but to disgrace and dishonor his enemies. "But the Lord is with me like a mighty warrior, so my persecutors will stumble and not prevail. They will fail and be thoroughly disgraced; their dishonor will never be forgotten" (Jer. 20:11).

These inspiring stories in the Bible show us how God used rejection to help and bless two completely different persons in their unique situations. And he can do this with us whenever we experience rejection. Not only can God heal our hearts, but He can use our pain for an intimate fellowship with him. Yes, some parts of us will die, but God will create and birth new ones.

He will impart humility, wisdom, fear of the Lord, and perseverance. Most of all, he will enlarge our souls to receive more of his unconditional love, so we may grow in compassion and empathy.

Declarations

- I know and rely on God's love.
- God is the lover of my soul, my ultimate satisfier, and the source of all my blessings.
- My value as a person is not dependent on my accomplishments and success. God continued to love me before and after the rejection of my work.
- Very often, rejection is God's way of protection and redirection in my life.
- God sees me and loves me always. I am valuable to him.

Losses and Gains

Losses When I Face Rejection
1. The loss of self-worth and self-confidence
2. The loss of peace
3. The loss of motivation
4. The loss of courage
5. The loss of a relationship
6. The loss of well-being and health

Gains When I Draw Near to God
1. The gain of spiritual growth and maturity
2. The gain of experiencing and trusting God's unconditional love and acceptance in Christ
3. The gain of humility
4. The gain of growing in the identity of a beloved child of God
5. The gain of wisdom and understanding
6. The gain of increased capacity to love God and others well
7. The gain of increased capacity for empathy and compassion
8. The gain of tested and purified motivation
9. The gain of growing in perseverance, self-discipline, and patience
10. The gain of strength and resilience
11. The gain of growing in the fear of God
12. The gain of freedom from the fear of man and people-pleasing tendencies
13. The gain of seeing and experiencing God in a deeper way as the one who sees me

Reflection Questions

1. What was the most painful rejection you have experienced? Why?
2. Do you tend to take rejections of your ideas or work projects personally? How does this affect you?

Meditation Verses

She gave this name to the Lord who spoke to her: "You are the God who sees me," for she said, "I have now seen the One who sees me" (Gen. 16:13).

"And so we know and rely on the love God has for us" (1 John 4:16).

"Do not be afraid; you will not be put to shame. Do not fear disgrace; you will not be humiliated" (Isa. 54:4).

"For your Maker is your husband—the Lord Almighty is his name—the Holy One of Israel is your Redeemer; he is called the God of all the earth. The Lord will call you back as if you were a wife deserted and distressed in spirit— a wife who married young, only to be rejected," says your God (Isa. 54:5-6).

"Dear friends, now we are children of God, and what we will be has not yet been made known. But we know that when Christ appears, we shall be like him, for we shall see him as he is" (1 John 3:2).

"As the Father has loved me, so have I loved you. Now remain in my love" (John 15:9).

"Am I now trying to win the approval of human beings, or of God? Or am I trying to please people? If I were still trying to please people, I would not be a servant of Christ" (Gal. 1:10).

"But the Lord is with me like a mighty warrior, so my persecutors will stumble and not prevail. They will fail and be thoroughly disgraced; their dishonor will never be forgotten" (Jer. 20:11).

*P*rayer

Dear Lord,

 Going through rejection feels like dying. I am struggling with lies bombarding my mind, and I doubt my worth as a person. Please, let me experience your unconditional love in a fresh way.

 Enlarge my soul and help me love you more. Enable me to love the people who hurt and reject me, too. Help me love others better without placing expectations on them that they can not fulfill.

 I declare now that you are my ultimate provider and satisfaction. You are the source of all my blessings.

 Heal me from the wounds of rejection and impart your blessings on me. Help me grow in the fear of the Lord and free me from people-pleasing tendencies.

 I want to see the one who sees me.

 In Jesus' name. Amen.

5

The Gifts Hidden in Loneliness

I hate to feel lonely. Unfortunately, after the unexpected loss of my husband and best friend several years ago, loneliness has been my constant companion. There is not a day when I don't struggle with loneliness. Even when I am surrounded by people, sometimes I feel this piercing pain of loneliness coupled with thoughts that nobody understands and cares about me.

The feeling of loneliness increases, especially on certain occasions like family celebrations, anniversaries, birthdays, and special days. I have a vivid memory of my first Christmas without my beloved. Nothing prepared me for the intensified pain and emptiness. I felt half of me was missing and I was walking around with my chest open and my tender heart shattered and exposed. My eyes kept darting, longing to see the one I missed so terribly. But the chair beside me was empty. The dazzling lights of the Christmas tree and the smiling faces of my friends gathered around the tree, laughing and spreading good vibes just magnified the incredible loneliness I felt.

I was thankful to be with them this Christmas, but I couldn't take part fully in their excitement and joy. The coldness in my stomach was heavy like a stone, and hot tears burned in my eyes.

I felt alone and unable to connect. We can have from time to time overwhelming feelings of loneliness. It becomes more traumatic when we feel this way for prolonged times and when loneliness turns into isolation and depression. But why is loneliness so painful?

I believe it is so excruciating because it hits right into the most profound need and longing God gave us. This is the need for authentic and intimate connection, bonding, and relationship. Yes, God has created us as relational beings, made in his image. The longing for connection has been encoded in our hearts and wired in our veins. We long to be seen, heard, understood, and loved.

Loneliness sends powerful and hurtful messages like:

Connection is impossible.
You are alone.
Nobody understands you.
Nobody really cares.
You are invisible.
You don't matter.
You don't deserve to be loved.

These messages are not necessarily true, but the real danger is when we internalize them. It seems loneliness deprives us of giving and receiving love, the most needed and powerful ingredient of life. That's why it damages the most vulnerable and needy part of our hearts.

Merriam-Webster dictionary defines lonely as "being without company, cut off from others, sad from being alone, producing a feeling of bleakness or desolation."[9] Here is how Wikipedia describes it: "Loneliness is an unpleasant emotional response to perceived isolation. Loneliness is also described as social pain – a psychological mechanism that motivates individuals to seek social connections. It is

---

[9] https://www.merriam-webster.com/dictionary/loneliness

often associated with a perceived lack of connection and intimacy."[10] According to Collins' dictionary, "loneliness is the unhappiness that is felt by someone because they do not have any friends or do not have anyone to talk to."[11]

Loneliness can be physical, emotional, and spiritual, and it affects us on all these levels. Interestingly, loneliness was one of the reasons God created a companion for Adam and made Eve. The Lord God said, "It is not good for the man to be alone. I will make a helper suitable for him" (Gen. 2:18). The phrase "a helper suitable for him" in Hebrew is "ezer kenegdo" and it is rich in meaning. The Hebrew word "ezer" carries the meaning of helper, companion, partner, indispensable pillar, and vision. It is also a word used in the Bible for God being our helper and supporter. The creation of Eve was God's wonderful provision for Adam's loneliness and aloneness. God gave him the gift of the companionship of a person suitable for him who could be his partner, friend, and become one flesh with him.

So, it is no surprise that one of the greatest losses loneliness brings is the loss of companionship, fellowship, and intimacy. It is also the loss of unity, the condition of being one with another person (one body and one mind) or being one spiritually. It is precisely this loss that brought me months and years of emptiness, numbness, sleepless nights, and a lot of tears after I lost my husband, my *ezer*. The soul is agonizing when it is separated and isolated from the source of love. We don't need to look further than the earthly life of Jesus and the point of greatest separation and isolation in his life. Jesus experienced the whole crushing burden of loneliness on the cross in the darkest moment when even the Father withdrew his presence from his son. This was something unimaginable, incomprehensible, and unthinkable.

Jesus' soul cry in Matthew 27:46, "Eli, Eli, lema sabachthani?" (which translates to *My God, my God, why have you forsaken me?*) can't

---

[10] https://en.wikipedia.org/wiki/Loneliness
[11] https://www.collinsdictionary.com/dictionary/english/loneliness

convey the misery and heartbreak of our Lord. Jesus experienced loneliness in his earthly life and ministry, but he always had the intimate closeness and fellowship of the Father. In fact, they were inseparable. That's why Jesus said, "I and the Father are one" (John 10:30). So, the loneliness Jesus experienced was caused by the deepest loss possible—the loss of the loving presence of God the Father. This loss was temporary but the gravest and most mortifying that someone can go through.

We see these same losses translating into isolation, separation, sadness, and abandonment in the lives of several other heroes of faith in the Bible, like Joseph, Daniel, David, and Paul. Their lives are marked by loneliness, yet there is a golden thread of blessings emerging from their agony. All of them accepted the invitation of loneliness and isolation to draw near to God. This courageous step of trust enabled them to unpack and enjoy the various gifts God had planned for them in some of the darkest periods of their lives.

Joseph and the Gift of Solitude

We are already familiar with Joseph's story in Genesis 37 and 38, but let's see it now through the prism of loneliness. Joseph came from a big family. As a child and teenager, he enjoyed the love and special attention of his parents, Jacob and Rachel. His father was very fond of him because he was the first-born child of his beloved wife, Rachel. This fatherly preference and love, however, stirred envy and hate in the hearts of his half-brothers.

The prophetic dream God gave Joseph symbolizing that one day his family and parents would bow down before him made this hatred explode. His half-brothers sold him as a slave in Egypt. There, he was falsely accused because he refused to compromise his integrity and was thrown in prison for a couple of years.

So, let's imagine this for a second. Joseph, a young boy, who used to enjoy the love and admiration of his parents, and their special treatment, suddenly finds himself in a foreign country, in a prison, cut off from everything familiar and all supporting relationships. Not only that, but his very own family betrayed him and wished him dead. He is completely alone, abandoned, and left to himself. There is nobody who can help him. Can you imagine the loneliness he might have experienced? He is truly in chains—in the physical prison chains and the emotional chains of loneliness. So, how has he survived these years of isolation?

We find the answer in the intimate bond he has developed with the Lord. The Word of God tells us twice that the Lord was with him. "The Lord was with Joseph so that he prospered, and he lived in the house of his Egyptian master" (Gen. 39:2). "But while Joseph was there in the prison, the Lord was with him; he showed him kindness and granted him favor in the eyes of the prison warden" (Gen.39:20-21).

Now, God is everywhere, and he is every moment with each of us. But here, the Bible implies something else. It is not just God's presence but Joseph abiding in this presence, finding strength in God's love, and trusting God's plan and purposes. How could he do this?

Joseph translated his time of being alone, lonely, and isolated into spending more time with God, without distractions. Being cut off from his family and normal routine, he spread deeper roots in God's presence and love. He had a lot of time in prison to think about all the events and the betrayal of his brothers. Instead, he learned how to listen to God's voice and let God comfort, strengthen, and help him. God gave him strength, wisdom, understanding, and success. It was even possible for Joseph to prosper in his circumstances simply because the Lord was with him, actively working in his life.

Joseph's first years in Egypt were marked by loneliness and solitude, but this was God's gift of special training, testing, and preparation to turn Joseph into the man and leader God called him to be.

Solitude and isolation were the best instruments to tune Joseph's heart to God's heart and make him ready for his mission and the blessings God had for him.

Daniel and the Gift of Purpose and Identity

We trace a similar pattern in the life of another great man—the prophet Daniel. In his youth, he was also cut off from everything known: his land, family, language, and way of life, future, and taken captive in Babylon. There he underwent a complete assimilation program and even his name was changed from Daniel to Belteshazzar (Dan. 1:7).

It is astounding, but it is exactly in this isolation and loneliness, and the extreme assault of his Jewish identity, that Daniel found God's gifts of purpose and identity. What made this possible? Again, we find the answer in Daniel's connection with God and his unwavering resolve to remain faithful to his God and not to defile himself. From the very beginning, he "resolved not to defile himself with the royal food and wine, and he asked the chief official for permission not to defile himself this way" (Dan. 1:8). God honored this decision and gave him and his three friends the favor and compassion of King Nebuchadnezzar. The Lord blessed these young people with "knowledge and understanding of all kinds of literature and learning. And Daniel could understand visions and dreams of all kinds" (Dan. 1:17).

Their integrity and decision to live as God's servants were tested many times in this hostile environment, but they remained unshakable. Even threatened with death, they didn't waver. The three friends of Daniel were thrown into the fiery furnace because they refused to fall down and worship the image of gold set up by the king. Daniel himself was thrown to the lions after he refused to change his daily habit of prayer and connection with God three times per day.

God rewarded his faithful servants exceedingly. He not only miraculously saved them from the fire and the lions, but he also vindicated and promoted them (Dan. 3:29-30). Most importantly, God's name was glorified and known. The king issued "a decree that in every part of my kingdom, people must fear and reverence the God of Daniel" (Dan 6:26). And "Daniel prospered during the reign of Darius and the reign of Cyrus the Persian." (Dan.6:28). What an amazing transformation! The people who wanted to assimilate Daniel and his friends, wiping out their Jewish identity and their purpose as God's servants through separation, isolation, and loneliness, ended with a command to worship the God of Daniel!

God honored and rewarded Daniel's choice to draw near to him, by giving him supernatural wisdom, understanding, and prophetic visions. He also promoted him and placed him in a leadership position and established him in his God-given identity and purpose. We see that God trains, prepares, and forms all his great leaders and servants in the trenches of isolation and loneliness when it is only them and God, cut from human support and safety networks.

The Greatest Gift of Loneliness

Loneliness can propel us straight into God's loving embrace. When we choose the path to the heart of God in our lonely hours and days, like Daniel and Joseph, we can taste the sweetness of God's nearness and intimate fellowship. We can enjoy the most precious gift of intimacy with the Lord. We can grow in the knowledge of the Lord, and wisdom and understanding, in our identity and purpose.

In this most lonely moment I had during my first Christmas without my husband, when I could not even express my pain and anguish in words, he heard the cry of my soul. I perceived this gentle voice in my thoughts, "I understand you, my child, and I deeply care." I came back home, and I invited Jesus in my loneliness and pain. Together we sat down, and I pulled out an empty Christmas card and wrote it to my husband, telling him how much I missed him. Then I mourned and sobbed in the everlasting arms of my Heavenly Father. Being open with him and sharing everything (the good, the bad, and the ugly) of our thoughts and feelings is one way to lean into his presence and build an intimate connection. We can intentionally have ongoing conversations aiming not only to share but also to tune our spiritual ears to hear from God. He is talking to us and longs to reveal his heart to us.

The most important truth to remember when we struggle with loneliness as believers is that God's presence is constantly with us and in us by the indwelling Holy Spirit. This means that we may feel lonely, but we are never truly alone. Even if we don't have a single person around us, we always have Jesus as our constant companion, guide, and best friend. We need to learn to walk with him and do life together with him and this is the greatest gift of loneliness.

Declarations

- I can use solitude and isolation to connect with God and listen to His voice without distractions.
- I may feel lonely, but I am never truly alone.
- God can strengthen and establish my purpose and identity in periods of loneliness and isolation.
- God allows loneliness to prepare me and help me connect deeper with him.
- Jesus is my constant companion, guide, and best friend.

Losses and Gains

Losses When I Face Loneliness
1. The loss of companionship and fellowship
2. The loss of friendship
3. The loss of intimacy
4. The loss of a relationship
5. The loss of joy and satisfaction
6. The loss of being cared for and supported

Gains When I Draw Near to God
1. The gain of spiritual growth and maturity
2. The gain of silence and solitude
3. The gain to commune with God and hear His voice without distractions
4. The gain of more time with God
5. The gain of intimacy with God
6. The gain of a deeper level of compassion and empathy
7. The gain of learning to depend on God and boast with Him
8. The gain of finding satisfaction, joy, and contentment in God
9. The gain of growing in wisdom, knowledge, and understanding
10. The gain of established purpose and identity
11. The gain of growing as a leader and servant of God

Reflection Questions

1. In which situations do you feel lonely?
2. What do you do to ease your loneliness?
3. Have you experienced God's nearness when lonely and how did this change you?

Meditation Verses

"You have made known to me the path of life; you will fill me with joy in your presence, with eternal pleasures at your right hand" (Ps. 16:11).

The Lord replied, "My Presence will go with you, and I will give you rest" (Exod. 33:14).

"Where can I go from your Spirit? Where can I flee from your presence?" (Ps. 139:7)

"And surely I am with you always, to the very end of the age" (Matt. 28:20)

"Don't you know that you yourselves are God's temple and that God's Spirit lives in you?" (1 Cor. 3:16)

"I am with you and will watch over you wherever you go, and I will bring you back to this land. I will not leave you until I have done what I have promised you" (Gen. 28:15).

"Here I am! I stand at the door and knock. If anyone hears my voice and opens the door, I will come in and eat with him, and he with me" (Rev. 3:20).

"Have I not commanded you? Be strong and courageous. Do not be terrified; do not be discouraged, for the Lord your God will be with you wherever you go" (Josh. 1:9).

"The Lord was with Joseph so that he prospered..." (Gen. 39:2).

Prayer

Dear Lord,

I feel so lonely. My words can't express exactly how empty, isolated, and unloved I feel. I crave close and warm relationships with other human beings. I long to be understood, seen, and heard. It would be wonderful to have somebody as a companion and friend.

I don't know what to do with these painful feelings. I bring them to you. Help me to sort them out and pour them out in your presence.

Lord, I declare that you are always with me. Even when I don't feel it and see it, I know this is true. Your presence surrounds me.

You know me intimately, Lord, better than I know myself. You are near, closer than any other human being.

Help me not to ease my loneliness with quick fixes. Please prevent me from making unhealthy choices such as overeating, drinking alcohol, and getting distracted by social media or TV.

I choose to face my pain and come with my loneliness to you. Please, do your intended work in my loneliness. Shape and form my heart, let me hear your voice, teach me, and share secrets with me. I want to receive your blessings and everything you have intended for me.

In Jesus' name. Amen.

6
The Gifts Hidden in Unmet Expectations

Expectations. Do you know that our life is built on them? Think about this for a minute.

The moment our feet hit the floor each morning, we enter the realm of expectations. We expect that our morning routine goes as usual without interruptions and surprises; we expect our bodies to function as they should; we expect the sun to rise and we expect the kids to behave.

Going through the day, we expect to manage our daily tasks and perhaps the day to run smoothly. We expect people to do what they say and keep their promises, at least most of the time. We expect our partners to love us and give us their attention and affection; we expect our friends to be there for us when we need them.

We expect to have a job (well-paid if possible), to own a house, to go on vacation, and to have fun. When we put our heads on the pillow, we expect to have a good night's sleep and to wake up refreshed.

We expect God to act in the way we have asked him, preferably now, and not after months or years. We expect him to give us what we want and to spare us from pain, loss, and discomfort, don't we? We expect fair and just treatment from God, people, and life in general. We expect. All the time.

It doesn't matter if we are conscious of our expectations or not.

But what exactly is an expectation? Merriam-Webster dictionary defines expectation as "the act or state of expecting: a looking forward to or waiting for something." This can be good or bad, but usually we expect good things to happen in the future. Here are several synonyms of expectations in the Thesaurus: assumption, confidence, hope, prediction, possibility, likelihood, promise, prospect, trust, assurance, expectancy, presumption, probability, reliance.

We see our expectations are a mix of assumptions and possibilities, but also a matter of confidence, hope, and trust. So, it is not a surprise that unmet expectations are and will be a major part of our lives. Unmet expectations towards ourselves, others, relationships, and life circumstances are the primary source of disappointment, anxiety, anger, and depression. How do we react when our expectations are not met? And why does it hurt so much?

Part of the answer is that expectations are based on desires. Expectations directed to God, people, and relationships relate to our desire for them to treat and love us and to meet our needs in a certain way. So, the core message of unmet expectations is:

You are not treated the way you should be.
You are not respected.
You are not loved.

But the truth is that our desires and expectations are always an expression of our basic attitudes, ideas, and beliefs. They show how we think about ourselves, life, relationships, marriage, friendship, happiness, God, etc.

Often, our expectations function as our own security, predictability, and control system. Therefore, when something does not develop according to what we expect, the system switches on an alarm. This throws us into a state of anxiety, confusion, and anger. We lose the control we think we have when people and situations do not correspond to our preconceived ideas and expectations. But we have control only over ourselves and our inner life, including our thoughts, feelings, and decisions. This is the most important type of control because it determines how we experience reality.

However, when a major expectation is not met, we face multiple painful losses like our idea of happiness, our plans, hopes, the fulfillment of dreams and wishes, and the feeling of joy, and satisfaction.

Perhaps the most cardinal loss is our happiness. As mentioned before, our expectations are focused mainly on awaiting something good to happen or things to go our way, the way we consider best. We want this good to happen because it contributes to our happiness and satisfaction. And who doesn't want to be happy? The unmet expectations based on good and even godly desires blow up our carefully constructed concept of how our lives should look like so we can be happy.

My idea of happiness was torn into pieces, when my expectation to have a normal family and become a mother didn't fulfill after years of trying and, despite strong beliefs, passionate prayers, and faith in God.

The shattering of the big pink balloon of how I imagined my life would look like actually was a chain of unmet expectations: big and small. This was my script:

- Marry the love of my life: *check!*
- Have a wonderful and passionate marriage: *no check!*
- He wants children: *no check!*
- My husband always understands me and is there for me: *no check!*
- The moment we decide to have children, it will happen: *no check!*
- The doctors will help us have children: *no check!*
- God will give us a child: *no check!*

What I imagined as a happy life just didn't happen. The building blocks of expectations and desires towards my body, my marriage, my husband and God didn't fit into place to build the palace I imagined. This all caused intense pain and anguish that pushed me into a generalized anxiety disorder, health problems, and depression. Yes, the losses were real, and it seemed they caused a lot of damage to my heart and body.

So why does God allow us to deal with so many unmet expectations? What are the gifts he wants to give us through these painful experiences?

Ruth and Naomi: Replacing Expectations with Expectancy

The book of Ruth in the Bible tells a beautiful and powerful story. Ruth is the main character of this story, together with her mother-in-law, Naomi. This is a multi-layered story about the beauty of friendship, companionship, love, and loyalty but also about God's redemption, providence, and far-reaching plans and blessings.

Let's look at this story through the prism of unmet expectations and the blessings God gave for both Ruth and Naomi.

Both women suffered severe blows that shattered their expectations for a good life. Naomi was a Jew, and she moved to the land of Moab with her husband and two sons to escape the famine in the land of Judah. There, her sons married Moabite women, one of them was Ruth.

What were Naomi's expectations? Surely, she expected a better life with enough food and a blessed family, and most probably grandsons and granddaughters from her sons. She left Judah for good, not for bad. But...her husband died and then both her sons died. What a tragedy! Her life fell completely apart, her expectations shattered to dust. She was now a widow, childless, in a foreign land, without grandchildren and any perspective for that. She turned homeless, poor, and without support. This tragedy shattered also her identity and the way she saw herself. This is the reason she even changed her name. "Don't call me Naomi," she told them. "Call me

Mara, because the Almighty has made my life very bitter. I went away full, but the Lord has brought me back empty. Why call me Naomi? The LORD has afflicted-me; the Almighty has brought misfortune upon me" (Ruth 1:20-2).

And what about Ruth? She married a Jew, a believer in God, but after ten years of marriage, she was left a childless widow too. This was the worst imaginable situation for a woman at that time. Widows and orphans were the most vulnerable social groups. That's why God took special care of these two groups in his law and gave some special instructions to ensure their safety and provision for them.

What were these women supposed to do? What expectations could they have more in life? Other husbands for the three of them? Other sons for Naomi? Unrealistic and hopeless.

But something else was born instead, and we find the key in Ruth 1:6, "When Naomi heard in Moab that the Lord had come to the aid of his people by providing food for them, she and her daughters-in-law prepared to return home from there." The Lord had come to the aid of his people. This stirred expectancy and fresh hope in the hearts of Naomi and Ruth. Ruth refused to leave her mother-in-law and accompanied her back to the land of Judah. The rest is history. Did God meet the expectations and hopes of these vulnerable women who trusted and had faith in him? Yes.

God exceeded any expectations they might have about his provision and help. He provided not only sustenance and a husband for Rut, but he provided a home and a position of honor for both Naomi *and* Ruth. Ruth gave birth to a son, and Naomi gained a grandson, and one in the family line of Jesus! God placed a Moabite woman in the lineage of the Messiah.

Only God can author such a beautiful story of redemption, restoration, and far-reaching, eternal blessings. The unmet expectations for a better and normal life turned Naomi temporarily into Mara, a bitter woman, but what a triumphant ending God gave her.

"The women said to Naomi: 'Praise be to the Lord, who this day has not left you without a guardian-redeemer. May he become famous throughout Israel! He will renew your life and sustain you in your old age. For your daughter-in-law, who loves you and who is better to you than seven sons, has given him birth'" (Ruth 4:15-16).

Not Depending on Our Expectations but on God

As we see in the story of Ruth and Naomi, one of the greatest gains of unmet expectations is to learn to depend not on our expectations, but on God.

God's will is to redirect us to a life that does not depend on the fulfillment of expectations. His will for us is a life that is oriented and depends only on him as the center and fulfillment of all human longings. He calls us to a life where our primary concern is how to please and honor him and not how to please ourselves by ensuring our expectations are met. An important aspect of this dependency is to learn to redirect our sense of security and safety to God.

We are clinging to our expectations, driven by the need to control things and people to ensure the fulfillment of our desires. God has called us to another path: to surrender our control to him. This is the path of humility and faith. This way is painful and destructive for the ego and pride. God desires he to become our source of security, protection, and provision.

God does not give us a guarantee for fulfilling our expectations and desires in life. He gives us just one guarantee and security—himself and his love. In Christ, through faith, we have constant access to him. He is always available and at our disposal. For those who seek and trust him, he guarantees joy, peace, and satisfaction in all circumstances, regardless of unmet expectations.

God's response to our unmet expectations and disappointments is his grace. It is the power and energy to persevere and even increase our joy and satisfaction, whatever happens. This is the ongoing transformation in the image of Christ, and the ability to humble ourselves. It is the power to live a responsible and free life. We learn not to measure our happiness by the number of met expectations or fulfilled desires, but by knowing God's grace and love.

Learning to Handle Responsibly Our Expectations

Another major benefit of unmet expectations is learning to handle expectations responsibly. Taking responsibility is part of becoming spiritually and emotionally mature.

There are several steps to handle our expectations responsibly. These are acknowledgment, re-adjustment, and communication of our expectations. We acknowledge our expectations when we know their source and learn to evaluate if they are realistic, acceptable, and reasonable. Very often, we have unrealistic expectations for ourselves, our lives, other people, and the world. These are expectations that do not consider reality and come from a wishful, idealistic notion. If needed, we also learn to readjust some of our expectations. We can benefit from having lower expectations for ourselves and others and accepting our weaknesses and experiences. God calls us not to judge, but to have compassion. "Accept one another, then, just as Christ accepted you, in order to bring praise to God" (Rom. 15:7).

God's word is the best means of testing and renewing our thinking. As a result, we can form new expectations based on the right perception of ourselves and life. "Do not conform to the pattern of this world, but be transformed by the renewing of your mind. Then you will be able to test and approve what God's will is—his good, pleasing and perfect will" (Rom. 12:2).

Finally, we can learn to communicate our expectations properly. People, even the closest, can't read our thoughts. When we have a specific expectation, and it is neither unrealistic nor unreasonable, it is necessary to share it in an appropriate, undemanding way. This enables the other person to decide if they can and/or want to meet our desires. "A gentle answer turns away wrath, but a harsh word stirs up anger!" (Prov. 15:1)

Unmet Expectations: Building Blocks of a Reconstructed Life

I am amazed by the way God used my unmet expectations of what a happy, married life would look like to deconstruct my life and then rebuild it to another shape.

He has shown me happiness, joy, and satisfaction are possible even when we don't get what we want and things don't happen as we plan them. I learned from experience that happiness is not in my hands; it is not mine to produce it and to control it.

My unmet expectations of becoming a mother and having the family I wanted were like sharp surgery instruments to peel off layers of my ego and self-focused life. They broke my soul into pieces, yes, but they also broke my preconceived scripts, ideas, and imaginations. They reached far down to my core identity and what I thought of myself and shattered this, too.

For a time, my life and my heart looked like a construction site full of debris and dust. The past was no more and what I wanted was not possible. And then I slowly began to see the work of God as the master builder and restorer. He cleaned, molded, reshaped, and rearranged the pieces of my life. A new pattern emerged, rooted in an unshakable and eternal foundation.

I didn't have the life I wanted. But I received a new heart, and a new life in which I was at peace, humbled, and full of joy. It was no longer about me, my desires, my ideas, and my expectations. The center of my life and happiness has shifted to the only one who is more than I will ever need in this lifetime.

Declarations

- Unmet expectations are and will be a major part of my life.
- My expectations are an expression of my basic attitudes, ideas, and beliefs. They indicate how I think about myself, life, relationships, marriage, friendship, happiness, God, etc.
- One of the greatest gains of unmet expectations is to learn to depend on God and put my hope in him.
- When I seek and trust God, he promises joy, peace, and satisfaction in all circumstances, regardless of my unmet expectations.
- My happiness is not measured by the number of met expectations or fulfilled desires, but by knowing God's love.

Losses and Gains

Losses When I Face Unmet Expectations
1. The loss of my idea of happiness
2. The loss of fulfilled desires and accomplished plans
3. The loss of fulfilled dreams
4. The loss of joy and satisfaction
5. The loss of sense of control and security
6. The loss of being loved and valued

Gains When I Draw Near to God
1. The gain of spiritual and emotional growth and maturity
2. The gain of learning to depend on God
3. The gain of redirecting my security from my expectations to God
4. The gain of happiness that doesn't depend on expectations
5. The gain of reshaped life concept of happiness
6. The gain of learning to handle responsibly my expectations

7. The gain of improved communication and relationships
8. The gain of acknowledging, readjusting, and communicating expectations
9. The gain of replacing expectations with expectancy and faith in God
10. The gain of finding satisfaction, joy, and contentment in God
11. The gain of surrender and humility
12. The gain of placing my hopes in God's kingdom and the restoration of all things
13. The gain of a reconstructed, God-focused life

Reflection Questions

1. What are your most painful unmet expectations? How did you deal with them?
2. What are your expectations of God?
3. What is your idea of happiness?

Meditation Verses

"All people are like grass, and all their faithfulness is like the flowers of the field. The grass withers and the flowers fall, but the word of our God endures forever" (Isa. 40:6-8).

"The thief comes only to steal and kill and destroy; I have come that they may have life, and have it to the full" (John 10:10).

"And God is able to bless you abundantly, so that in all things at all times, having all that you need, you will abound in every good work" (2 Cor. 9:8).

"Grace and peace be yours in abundance through the knowledge of God and of Jesus our Lord" (2 Pet. 1:2).

"Lord, I know that people's lives are not their own; it is not for them to direct their steps" (Jer. 10:23).

"For whoever wants to save their life will lose it, but whoever loses their life for me will save it" (Luke 9:24).

"Humble yourselves, therefore, under God's mighty hand, that he may lift you up in due time" (1 Pet. 5:6).

Prayer

Dear Lord,

I have so many unmet expectations. There are the daily minor ones and there are the big ones, which brought me so much disappointment and sadness. I want to be happy, Lord.

I release all my unmet expectations to you now and declare that my happiness is not in my hands. Please examine and adjust my idea and concept of happiness. Show me you are the giver of an abundant and satisfying life that is greater than any human concept of happiness.

Lead me in this abundant life. Use my unmet expectations as instruments to deconstruct my soul and life, purify and sanctify me, and reconstruct me in the image of Christ. Give me the life you have planned for me.

Free me from a self-centered life and help me live with you as my center and most passionate desire and aspiration.

In Jesus' name. Amen.

7
The Gifts Hidden in Disillusionment

I was devastated when the unimaginable happened in my life, despite my prayers and trust in God for my husband. It broke me. Until that point, despite receiving several times a "no" from God to different major prayer requests and burning desires, I could still see meaning and purpose. I could continue in peace, trusting God and waiting for his plan to unfold.

But I found no meaning in this. I couldn't understand. This made absolutely no sense. On a bright summer day, out of the blue, I was caught in a tornado that turned my world upside down and changed it forever.

On July 5, 2020, my beloved husband Thomas died. He was just 55. God didn't heal him and didn't save his life.

Nothing would have prepared me for the days preceding his death and this insurmountable loss. He didn't feel well one day and went to see a doctor who sent him for some blood tests. The tests showed he was about to experience a heart attack, so they ushered him into the hospital. They prepared him for emergency heart surgery that took the entire night. The operation succeeded and ended with four bypasses.

He started to bleed, however, and the doctors placed him into an artificial coma that lasted three days. They woke him and I was able to see him the day after. I was so grateful to God that Thomas was awake and recovering, and that I could visit him in the intensive care unit during the coronavirus pandemic. My heart overflowed with joy and thanksgiving after the agony of the last days. I went to see him a second time, not knowing this would be the last time I would see him alive. He laid there with closed eyes, holding my hand. From time to time, he opened his eyes, searching to see my face, and squeezing my hand. I will never forget the helpless look in his eyes. My heart was breaking.

The next morning, I received a call that he had fainted and was brought in for surgery again. After the surgery, they called to tell me they could not find the reason for his fainting. Soon after, I got another call that Thomas was bleeding again and would undergo yet another surgery. I was dying from worry and anguish. I could not eat or sleep, only pray for God to have mercy. After the last procedure, they placed him in another artificial coma. On the seventh day of this induced coma, I got a call, the type nobody wants to receive. They told me I needed to come to the hospital because they planned to stop life-support.

This was a day I would never forget, the worst in my life—the day I said goodbye, weeping over his disfigured, swollen body, connected to various machines. I told him he could let go, that it was okay, and that I would be okay. It didn't feel this way, though. I felt abandoned and betrayed by God.

Out of nowhere, I lost my husband, my friend, and my closest person. I lost my family, my cherished life in Austria, and was forced to undergo a series of painful transitions. I moved back to Bulgaria to be closer to my family and friends. A new, unwanted, and difficult life began—a life of loneliness, in the chains of grief, without a husband or children.

So many losses...in the months that followed, I realized this was the greatest test for my faith. Now it was time for me and everybody to see if my house was built on the rock or the sand. Will I sink or will I stand? The Holy Spirit had imprinted one word on my heart at the beginning of 2020: stand. Do you know when you need a warning to stand? When a storm is coming upon you.

The disillusionment eroded my faith in God as a good and just God. I lost my expectations for God to move, having passed through circumstances where God didn't move the mountains nor removed the burden. Passing through the valley of the shadow of death and life-altering loss, I lost my belief that God still does miracles or does the impossible. My confidence cracked.

Along the way, tiny cracks have opened in the foundation of my faith, pockets of doubt and unbelief, disillusionment, and cynical attitude. I sensed the poison in these cracks when "What's the point?" questions crossed my mind:

God will do what he pleases, so what's the point to ask? What's the point of seeking further? What's the point of continually knocking on the door?

I thought I was a strong believer. Nothing could shake my faith in God because God could never disappoint me. I knew who he was; I knew his character and his love. No, I would never struggle with disillusionment.

Until I did.

There are many forms of disillusionment, but one of the most painful, far-reaching, and crucial is the disillusionment of faith. It touches the deepest parts of your souls, the very foundation of our beings. It affects us mentally, emotionally, and spiritually.

What is disillusionment? It's defined as disappointment deriving from unmet expectations and perhaps mixed with our own anxiousness from being hit with reality. Disillusionment is a profound disappointment to the point of depression that shakes our beliefs and requires us to make changes. Disillusionment places us in a state of destruction and chaos as part of our major beliefs falter and perhaps even break. What shall we do? Shall we fight to strengthen them and make them unshakable, or shall we let them crumble to the ground and then build a new belief system?

This is such a raw, messy process, filled with a lot of doubts, questioning, confusion, and pain.

The process of testing and re-evaluating our beliefs is especially agonizing when God and what we believe about him turns out not to be as we believed. This puts our entire relationship with him at stake. If we choose to turn our backs on him and stop having fellowship as a result of the disillusionment, this would lead to the greatest loss that we could ever experience.

As with every death experience, disillusionment also has the power to make or break us. But if we hold on to God in this entire process of disintegration and rebuilding, we will surely receive some of the greatest blessings possible.

In my struggle with disillusionment, the book of Job and his struggles to keep his faith in a fair and just God resonated deeply with me.

Job's Disillusionment and the Blessing of Unshakable Faith

Nobody wants to be in the place of Job, and no one would ever want to. His losses were too much for any person to bear. Some researchers think Job is a cumulative character for all suffering people because it seems too incredible for a single person to suffer so many losses in such a short time.

Job is also the perfect example for someone struggling with disillusionment in faith. Not only did his whole life disintegrate, but his theology disintegrated, too. On top of this, God seemed silent and absent during this colossal struggle.

Job thought God wasn't acting in a way he expected and supposed God should act. Imagine this: Job trusted a good and just God his whole life. He knew God and had a genuine connection with him. He knew God was a holy and righteous God. The Bible tells us Job was blameless, upright, and he feared God (Job 1:1). That's why, for example, he sacrificed a burnt offering for each of his children, making amendments for a potential sin, as was his "regular custom" (Job 1:5).

Job led a life of genuine faith and trust in God. As a result, he experienced God's blessings. This led to the following axioms in Job's theology:

- A righteous life leads to blessings and prosperity (suffering excluded).
- Good things happen to good people, and bad things to bad people.
- Good people deserve good things.

Suddenly, this seemed no longer true. On top of the losses, Job faced a dilemma. He could not reconcile the concept of a just, fair, and loving God who gave unfair treatment to a righteous person. Why?

Job began his agonizing quest for answers. He didn't know he would need to adjust his beliefs and find new theological truths that reflect, much more accurately, the spiritual reality. He could not imagine he would experience a birth—a birth of a "new" Job, and a rebirth of faith, tested in fire and polished as gold.

During his quest, Job questioned nearly everything he believed in. He questioned himself and his behavior, but found nothing he was guilty of. He questioned his beliefs about the world, the fate of the just and the unrighteous, and most of all, he questioned the character of God and his ways of running the universe. In his monologues, he went from one extremity to the other.

The same person who claimed: "My Redeemer lives," also said: "I cry out to you, God, but you do not answer; I stand up, but you merely look at me. You turn on me ruthlessly; with the might of your hand you attack me. You snatch me up and drive me before the wind; you toss me about in the storm. I know you will bring me down to death, to the place appointed for all the living" (Job 30: 20–21).

Who is God and why did he treat Job this way? Why did he allow this tragedy? We likewise ask, Why does he test our faith and let us struggle with disillusionment?

Job didn't get answers; he got *the* answer. He had a personal encounter and conversation with God, during which God showed him he is God—the only one truly capable of creating and running the universe.

This was a humbling lesson about God's unfathomable wisdom, knowledge, power, sovereignty, and absolute authority over all creation, including Job's life. Yes, God knew what he was doing. He had a far-reaching purpose for Job and his suffering. He knew Job would struggle with disillusionment, but he also knew what would come out at the end.

Job's theology and faith emerged from the darkness, standing on several new, unshakable pillars.

God is God, and we are just limited human beings. He doesn't owe us an explanation. God is sovereign and has full authority over life, all creation, and death. He always has the last word. That's why we can trust him with everything.

God remains just and fair, and he has a special time reserved for judgment. When he allows bad things to happen to good people, he is refining and preparing them to partake in his glory and to receive his true, eternal blessings of knowing him intimately and beings shaped in his image.

God is also the God of healing, restoration, and resurrection. He values and will reward the mature, pure, tested, and tried faith.

Job passed his tests successfully. His faith emerged from the ashes of disillusionment stronger and unwavering. He experienced God's faithfulness and restorative power as he never did before. God gave him a new life, new fortune, other children, but above all, a new heart.

God blessed him more and gave him *twice* as much as he had before (Job 42:10, 12). Job's suffering was not in vain despite his enormous losses. Truly, God had the last word in his earthly life and for eternity.

The Path of Healing and Blessings

If you too question your theology and play with the "What's the point?" question, I get it. Eventually, we all get disillusioned to some extent in our faith. This disillusionment hinders us from approaching the throne of glory with boldness and confidence.

What I learned during my own struggle with disillusionment is that God longs to seal the cracks in our foundation with hope, comfort, and renewed strength. He wants to develop the faith to persevere.

The first step to healing is to acknowledge the disillusionment. Because it touches the very foundation of our faith, it is easier to pretend it does not exist. Admitting it, however, brings freedom and allows us to pursue healing. It opens the way for God's truth and grace to reach these poisonous pockets of doubt and hopelessness and heal them.

For me, a practical way to acknowledge the disillusionment was to write about how I felt and the thoughts and questions that bothered me. I also talked with a trusted friend, a believer in Jesus, and I allowed myself to vent my frustration, questions, and tears.

Unlike the other painful experiences, where we could more easily turn to God and ask him for healing and help, the disillusionment makes this step extremely challenging. We perceive God as the source of our hurt, but we need to turn to him as the source of our healing, too.

Can we still trust him to do this? This is the crux.

There are two ways to cross this gap. The first is to continue talking to him, without masks and pretense. He can handle all our hurt, questions, doubts, and accusations. The second way is to continue feeding our minds and hearts with biblical truth.

When we meditate on the truths in God's Word and make it personal, we actively put our trust in God once again. By the power of the Holy Spirit, our confidence that we will see the goodness of the Lord in the land of the living grows.

God will use our disillusionment for good if we allow him. He will make our hearts steadfast and secure, enabling us to trust him without fear of bad news, with rich and unshakable expectations to experience God's deliverance and love daily.

"They will have no fear of bad news; their hearts are steadfast, trusting in the Lord. Their hearts are secure, they will have no fear; in the end, they will look in triumph on their foes" (Ps. 112:7–8).

Declarations

- Disillusionment is an opportunity to examine my theology and make changes.
- God longs to seal the cracks in my faith foundation with hope, comfort, and renewed strength.
- The goal of every test and trial is to receive more blessings and good from the Lord. It is enlargement and preparation to partake in his glory.
- God always has the last word.

Losses and Gains

Losses When I Face Disillusionment
1. The loss of trust in my relationship with God
2. The loss of confidence in my convictions and beliefs
3. The loss of the belief that God still does miracles and still does the impossible
4. The loss of confidence that God still delivers
5. The loss of the the belief that God is just and fair
6. The loss of hope that things will get better
7. The loss of the sense of peace in believing

Gains When I Draw Near to God
1. The gain of spiritual and emotional growth and maturity
2. The gain of tested, perfected, and resilient faith
3. The gain of a greater revelation of God
4. The gain of a greater revelation of ourselves
5. The gain of lamenting
6. The gain of a new measure of freedom and healing
7. The gain of freedom to express my whole self in the presence of God
8. The gain of a tested and tried theology
9. The gain of an unshakable hope
10. The gain of a perfected testimony
11. The gain of humility
12. The gain of a stronger bond with God
13. The gain of preparation for bigger blessings and good from the Lord

Reflection Questions

1. Have you struggled with disillusionment in faith? What was the reason for this?
2. Which part of your theology was put to the test?
3. What changes in your thinking and relating did the struggle with disillusionment produce?

Meditation Verses

"He led you through the vast and dreadful wilderness, that thirsty and waterless land, with its venomous snakes and scorpions.
He brought you water out of hard rock. He gave you manna to eat in the wilderness, something your ancestors had never known, to humble and test you so that in the end it might go well with you" (Deut. 8:15–16).

"I know that you can do all things; no purpose of yours can be thwarted. You asked, 'Who is this that obscures my plans without knowledge?' Surely I spoke of things I did not understand, things too wonderful for me to know" (Job 42:1–2).

"These have come so that the proven genuineness of your faith—of greater worth than gold, which perishes even though refined by fire—may result in praise, glory and honor when Jesus Christ is revealed" (1 Pet. 1:7).

"Would you discredit my justice? Would you condemn me to justify yourself? Do you have an arm like God's, and can your voice thunder like his?" (Job 40:8–9).

"He is the Rock, his works are perfect, and all his ways are just. A faithful God who does no wrong, upright and just is he" (Deut. 32:4).

"Righteousness and justice are the foundation of your throne; love and faithfulness go before you. Blessed are those who have learned to acclaim you, who walk in the light of your presence, Lord" (Ps. 89:14–15).

Prayer

Dear Lord,

I have lost my expectation for you to move in my life. I have lost my belief that you still do miracles and the impossible. I have lost my confidence that you still deliver and still move mountains.

Please expose and heal the wounds through which the disillusionment has come. Help me replace the false assumptions with your truth. Help me believe what is true about you and your involvement in my life.

Find the cracks in the foundation of my faith and fill them with your grace and love. Instill in me fresh hope and perspective based on your Word. Cement the foundation of my faith and make it unshakable and pure as gold.

Give me a fresh revelation of your glory, love, and purpose in my life.

Help me see every obstacle overcome. Strengthen me to believe that you can do with me, in me, and through me, exceedingly above all I could ever ask and imagine.

Return to your rest, my soul, for the Lord has been good to you.

In Jesus' name. Amen.

8

The Gifts Hidden in Grief

The heavy grief enveloped me like a dark cloud, pressing on my chest and taking my breath away. I only desired to escape, to go somewhere far away in a distant land, away from the cloud, away from the pain.

Instead, I put on my shoes and walked along the streets without aim or direction. My head replayed scene after scene. I remembered the day in the hospital when I saw my husband alive for the last time. I will never forget the helpless look in his eyes, the shallowness of his breathing, and how desperately he held onto my hand. Most of the time he had his eyes closed, only to open them from time to time, searching to see my face, and faintly squeezing my hand. "I am here, my love, I am here," I whispered every time. I left the hospital with a heavy heart, with the notion that something terrible, unthinkable would happen.

Then the last memory: me crying desperately over his unrecognizable, swollen body, connected with a machine that pumped air in his lungs and kept his heart beating, with tubes in his mouth. I couldn't kiss his mouth because of the tubes. I hovered over his body, stroking his forehead and uttering, "I love you. It is okay, my love, you can go home, it is okay. I will be okay."

Draw Near

Except that I was not okay. His death plunged me into cold, suffocating darkness and I felt the waters closing over me. I cried desperately to God in anguish, with tears and sobs. It was a shock to discover I could still breathe underwater and that I was still alive. How was it possible that I still lived in a world without my beloved? I didn't want to.

I still don't want to. Yet I am learning to accept the reality and I am learning to grieve well in healthy ways. I am on a discovery journey, finding out that grief is not my enemy but a way to process losses and a path to healing and transformation.

If you are breathing and have been around for a while on this earth, then you surely have experienced various losses. The human response to losses is *grief*. It is a heavy mixture of sadness, sorrow, anger, anxiety, depression, and a painful longing for what we have lost. Grief envelops our hearts in a dark cloud, and sometimes it seems there is no light at all. We carry grief around like a burden that weighs heavily on our souls.

So many significant losses can bind us in the chains of grief, such as the loss of friendships and communities, freedom, health, employment or financial stability, normality, and dreams.

Losing a loved one, a relationship or the ability to do things we want are also powerful sources of grief.

One of the cumulative losses we experience after we have lost something precious, especially a person, is the loss of our anticipated future. With the loss, our future has been once and forever altered. Often we see just blackness in front of us, which triggers our anxiety. It is especially challenging to imagine and believe that something good awaits us in the future.

The American Psychological Association gives the following definition of grief:

> "Grief is the anguish experienced after significant loss, usually the death of a beloved person. Grief often includes physiological distress, separation, anxiety, confusion, yearning, obsessive dwelling on the past, and apprehension about the future. Intense

grief can become life-threatening through disruption of the immune system, self-neglect, and suicidal thoughts. Grief may also take the form of regret for something lost, remorse for something done, or sorrow for a mishap to oneself."[12]

As we see when we go through a death experience (losing something or somebody of significance), that affects us emotionally, mentally, physically, and spiritually. Grief impacts us on all levels, and it is crucial to embrace it and see its healing and transformational potential.

Very few of us were ever taught how to acknowledge and grieve our losses. When we fail to grieve losses, we miss out on an essential way that God wants to meet us. Like David and Job, we have an invitation to discover the treasures buried in grief and loss.

What are we supposed to do with our grief? How do we not drown in the cold, mighty waves but instead learn to ride them, letting them take us to another shore?

David and the Power of Lament

David is an example of how to pay attention to our grief and feel it freely before God. He experienced many significant losses in his life, both in the period before he succeeded to the throne and during his reign. David lost his safety and freedom, a dear friend, and two sons (one as an infant and the other as an adult). He showed us, especially through his beautiful psalms, how we can still praise God with emotional integrity.

This means we need to give God access to all aspects of our lives and all the corners of our hearts. No masks or secrets between us. This is difficult and quite painful at first. However, it is God's way of purifying, healing, renewing, and constantly refreshing us.

---

[12] https://www.apa.org/topics/grief

The hidden must be consciously revealed so it can be changed. Since we have free will, which God respects, our desire, permission, and invitation trigger God's transformational work in our hearts.

The psalms help us identify and express different, often conflicting, emotions and how to direct them towards God. These poems cover a wide range of naming and expressing emotions, clothing them with words and sending them up to the throne of God.

Approximately one-third of the psalms are lament psalms. These psalms express sorrow, deep pain, complaint, anguish, and mourning—all aspects of grief. There are forty-two individual psalms of lament and sixteen community or national psalms of lament.

Let's look at several psalms of lament. Listen to how David expresses his pain in Psalm 6: "Have mercy on me, Lord, for I am faint; heal me, Lord, for my bones are in agony. My soul is in deep anguish. How long, Lord, how long?" (Ps. 6:2 3) David never feared to feel and name his grief with the words "agony" and "anguish." He complained to the Lord, asking him "How long?" Then he continued in verses 6 and 7: "I am worn out from my groaning. All night long I flood my bed with weeping and drench my couch with tears. My eyes grow weak with sorrow; they fail because of all my foes."

Here is another powerful expression of physical and emotional pain: "I am feeble and utterly crushed; I groan in anguish of heart. All my longings lie open before you, Lord; my sighing is not hidden from you. My heart pounds, my strength fails me; even the light has gone from my eyes" (Ps. 38:8–10).

Here we find an expression of spiritual pain: "Why, Lord, do you stand far off? Why do you hide yourself in times of trouble?" (Ps. 10:1). To think of God as distant, cold, and not willing to help shows the spiritual turmoil and confusion going on in David's heart.

Biblical lament is powerful because it helps us unpack at least three blessings stored for us in the darkness. These are the blessings of being our true selves without masks, the blessing of experiencing

God as our safest person, and the blessing of enduring hope and unshakable faith.

Grief is a teacher. While lamenting and expressing our grief in the presence of God, the mask falls and we learn to be ourselves. We share our emotions and thoughts that are not only painful but also scary, and we do this without a filter. Being and expressing ourselves freely is a self-discovery journey that fosters intimacy. We bond with God on a much deeper level.

We also learn to know him as our safest person and the ultimate grief expert. Everybody dealing with grief knows the need to communicate with safe people who are able to understand, empathize, and be near. The safest person to whom we can express our grief is our Lord Jesus Christ, who is called "the man of sorrows and acquainted with grief" (Isa. 53:3). Jesus knows the depths of grief, can feel our pain, have great understanding, and show compassion for us. He is fully able to empathize because he knows experientially every trial and every kind of suffering (Heb. 4:15). Lament imprints on us a deeper revelation of God as our closest and safest person who knows us in and out and loves us completely and unconditionally.

The third treasure of grief is the gift of eternal hope, and a stronger faith in God as our healer and helper, restorer and redeemer. This follows naturally because lament is a beautiful progression from complaining and self-discovery to God-discovery. When God is present, hope and the potential for healing, growth, and new life remain. That's why biblical lament strikes a deeper note behind the painful torment: "But I trust in your unfailing love; my heart rejoices in your salvation" (Ps. 13:5).

Job and Waiting In Between on God

It's not possible to talk about grief and not mention Job—a righteous man who lived through inexplicable suffering. Job suffered many losses in a brief period: his children, fortune, and health. There is a lot to learn from Job in the way he handled his immense losses and grief, but perhaps the most striking lesson is how Job held tightly to God in the blinding, suffocating darkness.

When grief hits us, it's as if we are hit by a truck. We stumble into a state of shock, followed by chaos and confusion. It is dark; it is heavy. We can't see our way through, and we can't understand. We gasp for air and strength to make the next step. In this darkness, we start to question and doubt, first and foremost God, but also ourselves and our beliefs.

How can we handle this disorientation and in-between phase? What blessings has God prepared for us in this darkness and how can we find them?

The day after my husband died, I came across this verse in Job: "God has made my heart faint; the Almighty has terrified me. Yet I am not silenced by the darkness, by the thick darkness that covers my face" (Job 23:16–17).

This spoke straight to my heart. These words were God's acknowledgment of the terrible season I was passing through, but also his assurance that the darkness covering my face would not silence me. I would not turn my back to God but would continue to seek him and communicate with him, following the example of Job. More importantly, the terror of grief would not silence my testimony of faith, as Job's losses didn't destroy his faith in a just and loving God.

With my heart heavily bleeding, I couldn't imagine at that moment how this would be possible in my life, but I believed these words. He would help me trust him and wait for him in this confusing place of blackness in which the past and the expected future are forever gone.

Job became my inspiring example of a person lamenting in the in-between, foggy place, contending for his faith. He knew his faith and his testimony were extremely valuable. Somehow, despite all the pain, he trusted God would strengthen his faith and perfect him like gold: "But he knows the way that I take; when he has tested me, I will come forth as gold" (Job 23:10).

His faith was at stake, and he longed for an explanation.

Yet what he needed was not just an explanation, but a deeper revelation of the ultimate power, knowledge, and sovereignty of God: our creator, master, and ruler of the entire universe. This is what God gave him: not an explanation. No answers to the "why" questions. Not a reason. Not a glimpse of the future. Instead of answers, God gave him questions.

"Job, I'll ask the questions. Do you have the same knowledge and power as me? Were you there when I created the universe? Where were you when I hung the moon and named the stars? Where were you when I birthed the ocean and drew its boundary? Do you understand the mysteries of the earth?

Can you give orders to the clouds, the rain, and the snow? Do you know how to tame the wild animals? Can you humble the proud? Job, do you want to rule the universe for a minute? Come on, try to create at last one orchid or one snowflake, come on!"

Yes, God is perfectly able to rule the universe and we can trust him to rule our universe, too.

Grief enlarged Job's capacity to receive and contain this greater revelation of God. Listen to his words: "My ears had heard of you, but now my eyes have seen you. Therefore, I despise myself and repent in dust and ashes" (Job 42:5–6).

Now I see you, God.

Now I have a new sight, a new understanding, a resilient, and unshakable faith. My soul can contain more of you.

Grief Shapes Us Into Comforters and Encouragers

I encountered the same process of enlargement of my soul's capacity in my journey of grief.

A larger capacity to receive and contain a deeper revelation of God means a larger capacity to love others well. God's comfort and empathy flow like a river and fill the voids in our shattered hearts. They become softer, more compassionate, and tender so we can comfort others with the comfort we have received. We become mature lovers. "…who comforts us in all our troubles, so that we can comfort those in any trouble with the comfort we ourselves receive from God" (2 Cor. 1:4).

It is not an accident that in the Old Testament prophecies, the Lord Jesus Christ is called "the suffering servant" and "the wounded healer." We are also following his steps when we let grief enlarge our heart's capacity for empathy and love. "If we are distressed, it is for your comfort and salvation; if we are comforted, it is for your comfort, which produces in you patient endurance of the same sufferings we suffer" (2 Cor. 1:6).

Grief can mold us to be a gift for other people. It is meant to work in us and through us, to give us depth, maturity, and new ways of living and thinking. It creates a capacity to hold more of God and other people.

The Gift of Freedom and Healing

Grief can force us to grow in a new measure of freedom. Here are at least six areas where we can gain more freedom.

- **Freedom from Self-numbing Addictions**
  Heavy loss may lead to self-numbing addictions such as overeating, drinking, shopping, and excessive TV watching. We need to guard our hearts against this by resolving to feel the pain and finding healthy ways to express it, like lamenting or talking to safe people.

- **Freedom from Unhelpful Thought Patterns**
  When we are in pain, we can easily start viewing ourselves as victims of circumstances or people, which can lead to hopelessness and despair. We need to guard ourselves against negative thinking, not forgetting that our feelings of pain don't always tell the truth.

- **Freedom from Toxic People and Critical Influences**
  It's crucial for our healing to let go of toxic people and

critical influences. It's good to surround ourselves with safe persons who are able to empathize and sit together with us in our sorrow.

- **Freedom from Guilt, Shame, and Blame**
  It is not unusual, after experiencing a huge loss, to struggle with intense feelings of guilt, regret, and shame. What will help us is the choice to accept forgiveness and extend forgiveness. This way, we root out the weeds of bitterness and open the way for God's healing touch.

- **Freedom from the Past**
  It is helpful to realize and accept that the past is forever gone. We are not the same anymore and we will never again have the same life we had before the loss. We need to surrender this past so we can start living in the present and move forward while believing God is redeeming our loss and still has a good plan for us.

- **Freedom from Our Burdens**
  When we are in a season of grief and pain, so many things can become a burden, even daily life. The Lord calls us to unburden ourselves in his presence, laying our worries, cares, and burdens at his feet. He longs to give us peace and strength to walk on the road of transition, healing, and growth.

Declarations

- When I fail to grieve losses, I miss out on an essential way that God wants to meet me.
- Grief impacts me emotionally, mentally, spiritually, and physically. That's why it is crucial to embrace it and use its healing and transformational potential.
- When I lament and express my grief in the presence of God, I can be myself without a mask.
- The Lord Jesus Christ is my safest person and the ultimate grief expert. He is fully able to empathize because he knows experientially every trial and every kind of suffering.
- Grief can shape me into a comforter, encourager, and mature lover.
- Grief can help me grow in a new measure of freedom.

Losses and Gains

Losses When I Face Grief
1. The loss of a loved one
2. The loss of a relationship
3. The loss of friendship, companionship
4. The loss of freedom
5. The loss of the sense of normality
6. The loss of a treasured way of life
7. The loss of a source of security and joy
8. The loss of health
9. The loss of the ability to do things I want
10. The loss of the anticipated future

Gains When I Draw Near to God
1. The gain of spiritual and emotional growth and maturity
2. The gain of maturity in love and compassion
3. The gain of God's comfort, compassion, and intimate love

4. The gain of a greater revelation of God
5. The gain of a greater revelation of ourselves
6. The gain of learning to lament
7. The gain of a new measure of freedom and healing
8. The gain of freedom to express my whole self in the presence of God
9. The gain of God's strength, help, and provision
10. The gain of new and more positive ways of thinking and living
11. The gain of a tested and stronger faith
12. The gain of unshakable hope
13. The gain of a perfected testimony of faith
14. The gain of of humility
15. The gain of learning to grieve in healthy ways
16. The gain of a stronger bond with God

Reflection Questions

1. What is your most recent loss? How do you grieve?
2. Can you share one healthy and one unhealthy way of grieving?
3. Which psalm of lament can best express your feelings and emotions right now?

Meditation Verses

"Have mercy on me, Lord, for I am faint; heal me, Lord, for my bones are in agony. My soul is in deep anguish. How long, Lord, how long?" (Ps. 6:2–3)

"Why, Lord, do you stand far off? Why do you hide yourself in times of trouble?" (Ps. 10:1)

"God has made my heart faint; the Almighty has terrified me. Yet I am not silenced by the darkness, by the thick darkness that covers my face" (Job 23:16–17).

"But he knows the way that I take; when he has tested me, I will come forth as gold" (Job 23:10).

"...who comforts us in all our troubles, so that we can comfort those in any trouble with the comfort we ourselves receive from God" (2 Cor. 1:4).

"But I trust in your unfailing love; my heart rejoices in your salvation" (Ps. 13:5).

Prayer

Dear Lord,

Grief is so heavy and painful. I have difficulties naming and expressing all the emotions I feel. But I come with them in your presence to mourn my losses. Give me the words and help me share my heart openly with you without masks and pretense.

I come to you as my safest person, my comforter, and the ultimate grief expert. You know everything about agonizing grief. I can trust you with my grief and my losses.

Lord, heal my shattered heart. Help me hold on to you when I feel disoriented and confused. Lead me through this dark valley and help me see the sun again. I want to see you, Lord.

I declare your sovereignty over my life. Lead me into a greater measure of freedom and shape me into a comforter, encourager, and mature lover.

In Jesus' name. Amen.

9

The Gifts Hidden in Betrayal

If anyone would have suggested to me this scandalous idea, that betrayal could be a gift when my whole being recoiled from the painful repercussions of being dumped by my best friend of over twenty years, I would have called this person crazy. Yet with sufficient time passing and God's intensive healing work in my heart, I could gain a new understanding and thank God for this painful experience.

Let's see what happens when we experience betrayal. According to the Merriam-Webster dictionary, betrayal is "the act of betraying someone or something or the fact of being betrayed: violation of a person's trust or confidence, of a moral standard, etc."[13] According to another definition, betrayal means "an act of deliberate disloyalty," like when your friend told other people all your secrets.[14] Other synonyms of betrayal are backstabbing, disloyalty, treachery, dishonesty, sellout, treason, double-dealing.

The core of betrayal is a violation of trust and confidence. As such, betrayal can wreak havoc in our relationships.

---

[13] https://www.merriam-webster.com/dictionary/betrayal
[14] https://www.vocabulary.com/dictionary/betrayal

Betrayal can look like:

> *I put an end to our relationship.*
> *I love someone else.*
> *I don't want to see you again.*
> *Don't call me anymore or try to contact me.*
> *Your husband has a lover.*
> *You are no longer my best friend. I have found another.*
> *I don't want to be together with you anymore.*
> *I don't love you anymore.*

Chances are that you have already heard some of these phrases or their variations. When they come from loved ones like friends and family or from people we trust, without explanation or a good reason, they feel like a bomb hitting us straight in the heart, spreading debris all over for a lengthy time.

The first wave of betrayal is the shock wave. We are stunned; we don't understand. Then we replay the hurtful words or actions a thousand times in our minds, intensifying the sharp pain that overtakes our hearts and bodies. We look for explanations and rationalizations. "What did I say to deserve that? What did I do or didn't do to get backstabbed this way?" We long for answers and we leap into self-defense mode. Feeling misused and mistreated, we hurt to the core of our being. We yearn for vindication and often for reconciliation. As the losses keep piling up, we feel sad, angry, and anxious.

Processing My Story of Betrayal

One day, out of the blue (at least for me), I heard the incomprehensible words, "I put an end to our friendship." No explanation. No desire to meet or talk it over. This was a friendship that lasted over two decades. I invested so much time, energy, and love in this person. There were periods when I spent more time with her than with my husband! We shared our intimate thoughts and feelings; we comforted and encouraged each other; it seemed our hearts and minds had intertwined.

To say that I was shocked is too faint a word to describe it. It was like a sudden illness, sending rays of unrelenting pain into your chest and all over your body. Trying to figure it out drained my energy. My head spun with the lengthy, imaginary dialogues, in which I was trying to get an explanation or prove my point.

This painful experience rocked my core, self-confidence, and trust in people. I felt ashamed, as if something embarrassing and dirty happened to me, labeling me "not worthy to be a friend."

This anguish and the strong desire for vindication propelled me on a desperate search for God and his intervention. I spent hours in his Word and poured out my heart in prayer and sobs. Gaining understanding and relief was my urgent need. I also needed grace, the strength to forgive, and to accept the loss of our relationship.

As time passed, I was able to comprehend my losses that are common for every betrayal: the loss of trust and confidence (in people and/or God), the loss of self-confidence, and the desire to be close again with another person.

The question, "Why?" burns in us when we feel betrayed. We pose this question not only to the person who betrayed us (in real or mental dialogues); we pose it also to God, wondering why he allowed this to happen. I was no different.

At first, I chased God demanding to know why, but the more I drew near to him, the more my questions, requests, and prayers changed. I learned that betrayal is a powerful moment for our spiritual formation, enabling personal transformation and deeper fellowship with God.

It was a pivotal moment for me: tearing the idol of the best friend forever concept and embracing the truth that Jesus is my best friend. Yes, I can have close friends, but I have only one faithful friend who will never betray, abandon, or disappoint me.

Betrayal, as with every traumatic experience, can push us either away from God or straight into his loving arms. We can know that there is no better expert on betrayal than God. He has experienced it multiple times, and he knows all the agony and painful emotions caused by betrayal. He is also the only one who can heal our wounded hearts and restore our trust and confidence.

We can get a glimpse of God's emotions in response to the betrayal of the people of Judah in Jeremiah 3. Through the mouth of the prophet Jeremiah, the Lord compares the relationship between him and the people of Judah and Israel to a marriage where he is the husband and the people are his wife. He compares his wife to a prostitute with many lovers who has betrayed her husband and has defiled the marriage. That broke God's heart.

"But like a woman unfaithful to her husband, so you, Israel, have been unfaithful to me, declares the Lord" (Jer. 3:20).

Nevertheless, God still loves the unfaithful people and desires that they return to him so he can heal them.

"Return, faithless people; I will cure you of backsliding" (Jer. 3:22).

When you wonder if God knows how you feel when betrayed, remember our Lord Jesus and the betrayal of Judas. The Lord was betrayed by one of his close friends, one of the twelve chosen disciples and apostles, in whom he invested his time, efforts, teachings, and power to usher his kingdom.

However, Jesus still calls him "friend" (Matt. 26:50), and still washes his feet during the last supper immediately before the betrayal (John 13:1–15). There is no unforgiveness in him, not one gram of darkness. Friend, Jesus can enable you to push through the pain and agony and forgive wholeheartedly, too.

David and the Betrayals He Faced

David is, "a man after God's heart" (1 Sam. 13:14; Acts 13:22). We might think such a chosen and anointed person would be exempt from painful experiences. We find the opposite to be true. Not only David was not exempt from betrayal, but he also experienced multiple betrayals: from a superior, from a close friend, and a family member. Let's look closer at his response so we can recognize some gains and blessings that are buried in the betrayal and how we can spot them in our own lives.

The first betrayal David experienced was by King Saul. The prophet Samuel anointed David as the next king of Israel, succeeding Saul. This was enough to spur Saul's fear and rage, so he set a course of chasing David to take his life. Saul experienced only good from David before he turned against him. It was David who won a major Philistine battle by slaying the giant Goliath (1 Sam. 17:5–7; 18:5). David likewise played soothing music to Saul when an evil spirit sent by God tormented him (1 Sam. 9:16).

Even though David then married Saul's daughter Michal and became a close friend of Saul's son Jonathan, an intense rivalry developed between the young new general and the king. Saul plotted to kill him. David had little choice but to flee to enemy territory.

Let's imagine for a moment young David fleeing for his life, and feel his anguish, fear, and extreme disappointment. He was loyal to King Saul; he won military victories for him and soothed his spirit, and as a reward, Saul decided to kill him. David should have felt betrayed.

How did this affect his fellowship with God? David was not only running for his life, he was running straight into the arms of God, pouring out his heart, not holding anything back. He lamented, he complained, he felt anger and pain, and amidst this, he also worshiped and praised the Lord. David could push through the curtain of pain and life-threatening obstacles and see God sitting on the throne. This was his God: the God fully in control, the promise-keeper, the faithful One. Psalms 34, 52, 59, and 63 have captured his emotions while he ran from Saul.

David turned to God for help and was confident he would receive it. "I sought the Lord, and he answered me; he delivered me from all my fears. This poor man called, and the Lord heard him; he saved him out of all his troubles" (Ps. 34:4, 6). David believed firmly that he would survive that hardship and would thrive because of

God's goodness and faithfulness.

"But I am like an olive tree, flourishing in the house of God; I trust in God's unfailing love forever and ever. For what you have done I will always praise you in the presence of your faithful people. And I will hope in your name for your name is good" (Ps. 52:8–9).

David was confident that God would defend him and punish the traitors. "I have done no wrong, yet they are ready to attack me. Arise to help me; look on my plight! You, Lord God Almighty, you who are the God of Israel, rouse yourself to punish all the nations; show no mercy to wicked traitors" (Ps. 59:4–5).

David set his heart on these truths and, at the appointed time, God punished Saul and put an end to David's agony and hiding. David sat on the throne and reigned over all Israel for several decades, and he administered justice and equity for all his people (1 Chron. 18:14).

This was not the last betrayal in the life of King David. He experienced another betrayal from a close friend. Likely this was Ahithophel, his trusted counselor, who betrayed David during Absalom's rebellion. We have a glimpse of David's emotions and reaction in Psalm 55.

> "If an enemy were insulting me, I could endure it; if a foe were rising against me, I could hide. But it is you, a man like myself, my companion, my close friend, with whom I once enjoyed sweet fellowship at the house of God, as we walked about among the worshipers" (Ps. 55:13–14).

This betrayal was more painful compared to the first one because it came from someone David considered a close friend, a companion, and a fellow believer. David had a strong, intimate bond with this person—emotional, mental, and spiritual. Most probably, he shared his most intimate thoughts with his friend. That's why the emotional pain was so intense and difficult to endure.

But David knew what to do. Again, he turned to God, to his haven, to pour out his frustration and anguish, to ask and receive help and comfort. He did this continually, throughout the day, staying confident that because of God's protection and involvement, he would pass through this ordeal unharmed. "As for me, I call to God, and the Lord saves me. Evening, morning, and noon I cry out in distress, and he hears my voice. He rescues me unharmed from the battle waged against me, even though many oppose me" (Ps. 55:16–18).

The third and perhaps the most painful betrayal in the life of David was the betrayal of his son Absalom, the third and favorite son of his (2 Sam. 15:1–20:22). Absalom, impatient to become king himself, rebelled against his father, David, forcing him to flee Jerusalem. David was emotionally torn between preserving his throne and preserving the life of his rebellious son. He preserved his throne but lost his son, who was killed by one of David's generals. The pain caused by the death of his son was stronger than the pain of betrayal (2 Sam. 18:33).

David's reaction was to turn to the Lord, praying for his mercy and meditating on his excellences. He did this continually and consistently with unwavering confidence that he would experience God's help and comfort. "Bow down Your ear, O Lord, hear me; for I am poor and needy. Preserve my life, for I am holy; You are my God; Save Your servant who trusts in You! Be merciful to me, O Lord, for I cry to You all day long" (Ps. 86:1–3).

Why did God allow these multiple betrayals in the life of David? Why does he allow betrayals in our lives? How can God bless us in and through a betrayal?

Betrayal can push us away from God or can compel us to come near him. If we choose to come near to God, pouring our hearts in continuous prayer and hiding his truths in our hearts, then something beautiful and breathtaking emerges from the fire: another version of us, closer to the image of God, stronger, wiser, more empathic and compassionate, and more like Jesus. The fires of betrayal give us a unique opportunity to experience the nearness and friendship of Jesus, our best friend, the Lover of our souls, the betrayed who will never betray.

This is the most precious blessing hidden in the gift of betrayal: experiencing more of God and deep personal transformation. David was not the same man after Saul's betrayal. Out of the caves in the desert came a wiser and humbler man who knew how to wage war in faith and trust God in his pain and with his pain—a blessed survivor who, on his turn, would be a blessing for his people.

My gains from my experience with betrayal were deeper friendship and spiritual fellowship with my husband, changing my ideas about friendship and cultivating openness to other people and types of friendship.

Steps of the Healing Process

There are several steps in the healing process of our betrayed hearts. Each step moves us closer to God and brings his healing and power into our lives.

1. Acknowledging the feeling of being betrayed and lamenting. Psalm 55 is a wonderful example.
2. Acknowledging and mourning each separate loss.
3. Forgiving the one who betrayed us. God wants to show kindness when mistreated and not to harbor resentment and bitterness in our hearts.
4. Surrendering our cause and situation to God.
5. Praying for God's vindication and defense, for example, with the prayers in Psalm 7 and 9.
6. Declaring our trust in God.
7. Choosing not to despair because God is the God of resurrection and restoration and he knows the future.
8. Choosing to submit to God's molding and shaping, and allowing him to bring all blessings and gifts hidden in this painful experience.

Declarations

- God loves me. I choose to trust the reason the betrayal is happening. I trust his plan and purpose.
- I am asking God for help, and I am confident that he will give me what I need.
- I will survive the betrayal and I will thrive because of God's goodness and faithfulness.
- I will draw near to God and allow him to bring all the blessings and gifts hidden in this painful experience.

Losses and Gains

Losses When I Face Betrayal
1. The loss of trust and confidence (in people and/or God)
2. The loss of self-confidence
3. The loss of the desire to love again and be open with another person and/or God
4. The loss of a relationship or friendship
5. The loss of fellowship in Christ

Gains When I Draw Near to God
1. The gain of personal transformation in the image of Christ
2. The gain of Increased capacity to receive God's comfort and to give such comfort
3. The gain of new revelations
4. The gain of a deeper level of intimacy with God
5. The gain of wisdom
6. The gain of freedom from the fear of man
7. The gain of an increased capacity to trust God

8. The gain of training in forgiveness and humility
9. The gain of freedom from the idol of friendship
10. The gain of new, healthier relationships and friendships

Reflection Questions

1. Why do you feel betrayed and who has betrayed you?
2. What is your greatest loss?
3. What and whom do you need to forgive?

Meditation Verses

"I sought the Lord, and he answered me; he delivered me from all my fears. This poor man called, and the Lord heard him; he saved him out of all his troubles" (Ps. 34:4, 6).

"I have done no wrong, yet they are ready to attack me. Arise to help me; look on my plight! You, Lord God Almighty, you who are the God of Israel, rouse yourself to punish all the nations; show no mercy to wicked traitors" (Ps. 59:4–5).

"But I am like an olive tree, flourishing in the house of God; I trust in God's unfailing love forever and ever. For what you have done I will always praise you in the presence of your faithful people. And I will hope in your name for your name is good" (Ps. 52:8–9).

"Cast your cares on the Lord and he will sustain you; he will never let the righteous be shaken. But you, God, will bring down the wicked into the pit of decay; the bloodthirsty and deceitful will not live out half their days. But as for me, I trust in you" (Ps. 55:22–23).

Prayer

Dear Lord,

    I feel betrayed by... It hurts so much, Lord. I fear I am losing... Please heal my heart. I decide now to forgive... for... in the name of Jesus. Clean my heart from any bitterness and resentment and help me continue to come to you and pour out my pain.

    I ask you to defend my cause and vindicate me in your time and way. I trust you, your plans and purpose. You are the God of resurrection and restoration, and you plan to give me a future and hope. I submit now to your molding and shaping and allow you to bring all blessings and gifts hidden in this painful experience.

    In Jesus' name. Amen.

10
The Gifts Hidden in Broken Dreams

Did you have a dream, and it came to nothing? Did you spend hours, days, months, or perhaps years chasing a dream and working to make it true, only to experience it crumbling to the ground and turning to dust?

The death of a dream is a painful experience. God made us to dream. He instilled in us a desire to reach for the stars, to pursue something beyond our control, and to passionately make sacrifices to achieve it.

According to the Merriam-Webster Dictionary, a dream is "something notable for its beauty, excellence, or enjoyable quality," "a strongly desired goal or purpose," and "something that fully satisfies a wish: ideal".[15]

Dreams are precious because they are part of the divine language. God often uses the language of dreams to speak to our souls and direct them toward something greater than ourselves. Dreams also contain a component of impossibility. We need divine interference to fulfill them. They teach us to believe and seek God.

---

[15] https://www.merriam-webster.com/dictionary/dream

Dreams are a powerful instrument of self-discovery. They help us find and understand our purpose, destiny, and mission—what we are created for. Having a dream is like having a fire in the heart that spurs us toward new, uncharted territory and motivates us to overcome all the difficulties on the road. Following our dreams leads us to a life of adventures and surprises.

God is the giver of dreams, and he is also the one who can make them come true. He is the giver and fulfiller of dreams.

It is important to say "yes" to the God-inspired dreams and visions within us. But we need to submit their fulfillment, both how and when they will happen, to the one who initiated them. God usually gives us such dreams and visions that far outweigh our capacity and resources. Only he is able to bring them to fulfillment in us, through us, and with us. It is important for us to understand, accept, and acknowledge God's ways and hand over the steering wheel to God.

God's Word tells us he fulfills the desires of those who fear him, and that fulfilled desires and goals are a tree of life (Prov. 13:12). Of course, this is not about selfish desires and egocentric passions, but about real, God-inspired dreams and visions.

How does it feel when this tree of life of strongly desired goals is cut to the ground? Instead of life, we face death with all its repercussions. We struggle with multiple losses and we don't know how to move forward.

Broken dreams inflict deep wounds on our hearts. The death of a dream is like the epicenter of an earthquake that radiates powerful waves of pain, failure, disappointment, anger, sadness, confusion, anxiety, and hopelessness. I remember well the day when one of my greatest dreams died, but it took me months to sort through and realize all the accompanying losses.

Since the beginning of my marriage, I wanted to become a mother. I thought this was the missing part of my identity and purpose on this earth. Having a child seemed to hold the answer to the void I felt. I dedicated myself to the fulfillment of this dream and started walking down the steep and rocky road. There were so many obstacles and roadblocks on the way—a reluctant husband, my decreasing fertility, bad medical reports, painful medical procedures, and a failed insemination attempt. And the last attempt: an in-vitro procedure with a donor egg.

I never came as close to my dream as I did in May 2015 with two implanted embryos in my uterus. This time I would surely get pregnant, I thought. In a blink, the day of the truth came. It took just a few minutes to take the pregnancy test. I was so afraid to look at it, so when I finally did, my brain refused to accept what my eyes saw.

This couldn't be true! With all the energy drained from my body, I had no wish to talk to anybody. The shock waves built a high prison around my heart, silencing the outer world. And it was such a gorgeous spring day! Nature showed itself in its splendor, bursting with joy and life while my life was sucked out of me.

I couldn't understand why God crushed my dream and left me a barren woman, unable to produce life. The more I chased my dream, the more tears and blood I poured into it, and the more elusive it became until I held nothing but broken pieces.

> *The broken pieces of my expectations of happiness and fulfillment.*
> *The broken pieces of my trust in God.*
> *The broken pieces of my hopes.*
> *The broken pieces of my joy and satisfaction.*
> *The broken pieces of my desired identity, self-realization, and self-validation.*

What was the value of these broken pieces? Why did God answer my fervent prayers with a "no"? Could it be possible that this was his way of blessing me by giving me something else instead?

Redirecting Dreams and the Birth of a New Identity

I sat in the ashes with the broken pieces of what I thought would bring me happiness and fulfillment.

By shattering my greatest dream in this period of my life, God shattered my heart, but not with the intent to destroy it. He aimed to mend it and redirect it. Every shattered piece, every debris, needed to be cleaned, re-shaped, and then put together again by the God of restoration.

One large broken piece was my search for happiness. I had made my dream of becoming a mother a condition for a fulfilled life. Becoming a mother had turned into an idol. My beautiful dream had morphed into an ugly monster called controlling desire. In the center of my thoughts and aspirations was not God (although I wanted him), but the idol of motherhood.

There was not a day, an hour, in at least five years in my life, when I had not thought about this. This desire was the filter through which I perceived everything. It dictated my value, happiness, and peace. The fulfillment of this dream was my chief motivation and driving force for a long time. It blinded me and controlled me.

How could you know that something has turned into an idol? You can know this by the space it occupies in your heart and mind. If it takes all the space and you can't imagine having a life without this thing or person, then you are in serious trouble.

God is a jealous God who is at war with the idols in our hearts. Sadly, even something as good and beautiful as a dream can turn into idol and rob us of our freedom and peace.

In the process of chasing my dream, I proudly believed I could control the world and guarantee the fulfillment of my wishes one way or another.

This, of course, was a deception. I refused to take a "no" for an answer. I didn't give God the right to answer my wishes and prayers as he desired. I didn't acknowledge him as God and ruler of my life.

God tenderly took this broken piece of my dream and laced it with the truth. He and only he is the giver and author of genuine satisfaction, fulfillment, and abundant life. It is not the fulfillment of wishes, dreams, and expectations that satisfies us.

God is bigger than that; even if he strips us of anything and anyone that we hold dear, we can still have the life he promised.

God satisfies our true needs and longings through Christ. God's invitation for me was to redirect to him my dream to birth life and be fruitful. I needed to place him in the center of my being, like an ocean that all the currents of my dreams were flowing into. Then and only then could I have peace and freedom. Only then I could trust God with my dreams.

When I realized it was not just about me—my ways, my needs, my desires, and my pleasures—I was able to humble myself and surrender.

Surrendering to God is a powerful process that enables us to wait for his action and intervention without fretting, worrying, or striving. We don't feel tempted to take matters into our hands. We can wait with peace to experience his plan unfolding at the right time. What a precious blessing!

When we do that, we reap a golden harvest. God gives us only the things for which we are ready and can steward without being crushed under their weight.

God surely fulfills dreams, but as God, he claims for himself the right to judge how, when, and in what form those dreams are fulfilled. He alone can do it best because he has unlimited knowledge, wisdom, and strength, and above all, unlimited, everlasting, and unchangeable love for us.

When I look back, I am thankful that God didn't give me a biological child, especially in the light of what came upon me just a couple of years later: the loss of my husband, moving to another country, and a major transition in life.

He knows me completely. He knows what the best is for me and how to bring his purposes to fulfillment in my life, taking into consideration my desires and dreams.

The dream of a biological child died, but the dream of motherhood lived. It remained, but I allowed God to redefine it and embraced his ways of fulfilling this dream. I committed myself to his call to mother others, and with his help I gave birth to a ministry and a writing career, and I poured my love into the children who were already present in my life.

Once I thought being a biological mother was the missing piece that would give me a sense of being successful in life, of having value. But this was a false foundation for my identity. I held a broken piece of misplaced identity in my hands, but God took it and gave me another piece, made from solid, unbreakable rock. I am his and he is mine. Nothing and nobody can change that.

Not my appearance. Not my health. Not my marital status. Not if I have children or not. Not my success. Not my failure. Not my fears. Not my possessions. Not my happiness. Not my sorrows. Not my life. Not my death. I am and will always be precious in his sight, purchased with His blood.

"For if we live, we live to the Lord, and if we die, we die to the Lord. So then, whether we live or whether we die, we are the Lord's" (Rom. 14:8).

How God Transforms Broken Dreams

There are a lot of examples in the Bible about God transforming shattered dreams and giving the dreamer much more in the process.

One of the brightest examples is the life of the apostle Paul. Two times in his life, God shattered his dreams and aspirations. The first was his dream to have a successful career as a zealous Pharisee and teacher of the Law. In Jewish society, the Pharisees were highly respected leaders. They held a position of religious authority and had the reputation of being holy men who kept the law and lived lives pleasing God.

Here is how Paul describes himself before his conversion: "circumcised on the eighth day, of the people of Israel, of the tribe of Benjamin, a Hebrew of Hebrews; in regard to the law, a Pharisee; as for zeal, persecuting the church; as for righteousness based on the law, faultless" (Phil. 3:5-6).

Paul's greatest desire was to please God, but the life of a Pharisee was the wrong way for him to do so. After his miraculous encounter with Christ on the road to Damascus, Paul's aspirations changed radically. Listen to his words: "What is more, I consider everything a loss because of the surpassing worth of knowing Christ Jesus my Lord, for whose sake I have lost all things. I consider them garbage, that I may gain Christ" (Phil. 3:8).

Amazing transformation! Still, as an apostle of Christ and a person who deeply loved the Jewish people, Paul wanted nothing more than to bring them the Good News. The salvation of his own people, his blood and flesh, became his dream and burning desire: "Brothers and sisters, my heart's desire and prayer to God for the Israelites is that they may be saved" (Rom. 10:1).

Again, he suffered bitter disappointment and rejection. Listen to his pain: "I have great sorrow and unceasing anguish in my heart. For I could wish that I myself were cursed and cut off from Christ for the sake of my people, those of my own race" (Rom. 9:2-3).

God had other plans and made him instead an apostle to the Gentiles, spreading the news about God's salvation to other nations and changing the world forever. Although Paul's dream was broken, God gave him the wisdom and vision to see that it was not over and that there was still hope: an eternal hope, beyond his lifetime, rooted in God's promises and faithfulness:

> "Inasmuch as I am the apostle to the Gentiles, I take pride in my ministry hoping I may somehow arouse my own people to envy and save some of them. For if their rejection brought reconciliation to the world, what will their acceptance be but life from the dead?" (Rom. 11:13-15)

Paul's dream was to live a life that pleased God and to see the salvation of Israel. God fulfilled this dream (partly), although not in the ways Paul envisioned, and gave the apostle supernatural understanding, wisdom, and peace.

May we all have this same attitude when we consider our broken dreams:

> "Oh, the depth of the riches of the wisdom and knowledge of God! How unsearchable his judgments, and his paths beyond tracing out! Who has known the mind of the Lord? Or who has been his counselor? Who has ever given to God, that God should repay them? For from him and through him and for him are all things. To him be the glory forever! Amen" (Rom. 11:33-36).

May we give glory to God who remains sovereign, doing immeasurably more than we can ask for and imagine.

Declarations

- My dreams are a powerful instrument of self- and God-discovery.
- I submit the fulfillment of my dreams, both how and when they will happen, to God as the giver and fulfiller of dreams.
- Broken dreams are God's way to mend and redirect my heart.
- When my dreams are shattered, God remains sovereign, doing immeasurably more than I can ask for and imagine.
- All my longings, desires, and dreams will find their fulfillment in Christ and his kingdom.

Losses and Gains

Losses When I Face Broken Dreams
1. The loss of my ideas and expectations of happiness
2. The loss of hope of receiving what I strongly desire
3. The loss of joy and satisfaction
4. The loss of the sense of self-realization and self-validation

5. The loss of trust in God as the giver
6. The loss of identity tied to the dream

Gains When I Draw Near to God
1. The gain of spiritual and emotional growth and maturity
2. The gain of Identity rooted solely in Christ
3. The gain of a new level of trust in God's sovereignty and wisdom
4. The gain of humility and dying to self
5. The gain of freedom from measuring up
6. The gain of investing my hopes in God
7. The gain of of finding greater satisfaction and joy in my relationship with God
8. The gain of a new beginning
9. The gain of knowing God as the God of restoration and resurrection
10. The gain of making God my greatest dream
11. The gain of learning dependence on God
12. The gain of finding my happiness in God
13. The gain of learning to wait on the Lord

Reflection Questions

1. Do you have a dream that didn't come true? How did you feel about that?
2. What is your greatest dream now? Why?
3. Did God fulfill a dream in your life in a completely different way and time as you thought?

Meditation Verses

"Hope deferred makes the heart sick, but a longing fulfilled is a tree of life" (Prov. 13:12).

"Do not worship any other god, for the Lord, whose name is Jealous, is a jealous God" (Exod. 34:14).

"The thief comes only to steal and kill and destroy; I have come that they may have life, and have it to the full" (John 10:10).

"All my fountains are in you" (Ps. 87:7).

"For if we live, we live to the Lord, and if we die, we die to the Lord. So then, whether we live or whether we die, we are the Lord's" (Rom. 14:8).

"My beloved is mine and I am his" (Song of Songs 2:16).

"Since you are precious and honored in my sight, and because I love you, I will give people in exchange for you, nations in exchange for your life" (Isa. 43:4).

"Oh, the depth of the riches of the wisdom and knowledge of God! How unsearchable his judgments, and his paths beyond tracing out! Who has known the mind of the Lord? Or who has been his counselor? Who has ever given to God, that God should repay them? For from him and through him and for him are all things. To him be the glory forever! Amen" (Rom. 11:33-36).

*P*rayer

Dear Lord,

I had a dream and now I hold only broken pieces in my hands. I invested so much time, effort, and prayers, and it came to nothing.

Lord, it hurts. It is not in my power to fulfill this dream or any of my other dreams. I humble myself before you and surrender my broken dream to you. Lord, if this dream I from you, resurrect it and make it true in the shape and time you see best.

You know the deepest and truest longings of my heart. Lord, increase my desire and passion for you. I want you to become my greatest dream and aspiration.

Help me trust your unfathomable knowledge, wisdom, and sovereignty. I declare that you can and will do immeasurably more than I can ask for and imagine, working with the pieces of my broken dreams.

In Jesus' name. Amen.

11

The Gifts Hidden in Hopelessness

Have you struggled with hopelessness or depression in your life?

It is normal for most people to experience brief episodes of depression. Many struggle with prolonged clinical depression and anxiety. Facing depression and mental health problems is common for non-believers and believers alike. Of course, the reasons are different, and how people handle depression and feelings of hopelessness varies.

Hopelessness is the prevailing component of depression. Usually, depression is characterized by a triad of hopelessness, worthlessness, and helplessness. The APA Dictionary of Psychology defines hopelessness as "the feeling that one will not experience positive emotions or an improvement in one's condition. Hopelessness is common in severe major depressive episodes and other depressive disorders and is often implicated in suicides and attempted suicides."[16]

I can count at least three periods in my life marked by prolonged hopelessness and depression.

---

[16] https://dictionary.apa.org/hopelessness

The first period was in my teens. Living in an atmosphere of fear because of the abusive behavior of my father, I sank deep into a pit of depression, self-doubt, and suicidal thoughts. By this time, I had already discovered the huge discrepancy between what I wanted to be and what I was, and my absolute inability to change my condition. I was terrified and ashamed of certain thoughts and actions that I was not able to change. This became a perpetual source of hopelessness. Life seemed void of meaning and purpose. My soul was thirsty for unconditional love and belonging, for something stable and secure.

I desired to be good, but I couldn't. I wanted to love, but I couldn't. A hurricane of resentment, offense, hatred, and anger raged uncontrollably within me.

In utter desperation, I cried out to the universe and placed an ultimatum. "God, if you exist, I challenge you to show yourself to me. Otherwise, there is no reason for me to live anymore."

I was looking for a way, a truth, and life. I was looking everywhere, hungry for something more than what my eyes could see, reading books about all religions, trying to touch the truth and fill the void. The country I lived in was still a communist state at that time, and my family was not religious. The only exception was my grandmother.

Sometimes, when I was a child, she would give me a small, shabby book for me to read. I could not understand what I was reading. But I had a favorite part at the end of the book. I cried in my need for somebody who "will wipe every tear from [my] eyes," and for a time when "there will be no more death or mourning or crying or pain, for the old order of things has passed away" (Rev. 21:4).

In my most desperate time, God found me. Through a series of coincidences and divine appointments with people who knew Jesus, I heard the Gospel for the first time and experienced a dramatic encounter with God and his love. The realization that I have a heavenly Father who loves me unconditionally and who will never abuse me or control me but instead support and encourage me till the end, became a fountain of life to me. It pulled me back from the edge of the pit I was about to throw myself into and gave me a reason to live.

This was the first time I discovered that depression could be transformed into godly sorrow and lead me to repentance and submission to God.

"Godly sorrow brings repentance that leads to salvation and leaves no regret, but worldly sorrow brings death" (2 Cor. 7:10).

Every form of depression and hopelessness contains an element of godly sorrow—this ache for the one thing that can truly satisfy.

My longing for God and the joy of following him were the reasons for my second round of depression in my thirties. I was happily married to the love of my life and best friend; I had an interesting and well-paying job; we enjoyed a good and comfortable life in a beautiful country, but . . . There is always a "but", isn't there?

The surface of my "but" was my unsatisfied desire for a child. However, under the longing for a child, another, stronger yearning was taking form, birthed from sorrow and depression. A long-forgotten yearning for something or somebody I once had. Unable to suppress it anymore, I confessed it. I was mourning my lost relationship with God and was longing for him, for the one I turned my back on many years prior.

It persisted for a long time, but the longing and the memories only grew stronger. There was the gnawing pain, and there was the cure: to reconnect with him again.

But how could I do that? I neglected him for so many years. He felt so distant and unapproachable, like the bright stars in the night sky. The only step I could come up with was to read the Bible from the beginning to the end. It felt awkward, and though I was reading and praying a little every day, the genuine connection was still missing. I lacked understanding, and often the words remained covered and cold.

But I kept going because I knew that fellowship with Jesus was the way out of my hopelessness and depression. Again, depression paved the way for my return to God.

Two times, God used my hopelessness and depression as a birth canal for the greatest blessing possible. This is the blessing of initiating and then restoring my relationship with him, giving me unrestricted access to him and his love.

The third round of depression was of another kind and had a different reason. I already had a good connection with the Lord and was committed to follow him faithfully. My life had a solid foundation, and I was stretching roots in the eternal Rock.

Then death came like a hurricane that shook my foundation, intending to uproot me. Depression and hopelessness followed death on the heels. This time, the source of my depression was a trust issue. Could I continue to follow and trust a God who allowed the premature death of my beloved and took away my family and everything I treasured? Could I still trust him when he led me into the valley of the shadow of death? Was he still good? Did he still love me? Did I truly know him, or did I just follow my ideas about him? Was it safe for me to trust him?

Questions, questions, questions birthed from the pain and the struggle to keep my faith and hope alive.

This time, depression was a tool God used to test my beliefs and the foundation of my faith. There was a way back again into the embrace of the eternal arms: humbly accepting his mysterious ways. This was a way leading to a tested and perfected faith and a new, resilient hope.

The Prophet Jeremiah and the Delusion of Hopelessness

Many godly people in the Bible struggled with episodes of hopelessness and depression in the face of extreme circumstances. One bright example is the prophet Jeremiah. He had a hard life, living in a very special moment of history, prophesying and awaiting the impending doom of his nation. His present was challenging, and the future was bleak: destruction by the Babylonians and exile to a foreign nation!

It is natural to feel hopeless and depressed when you know nothing good is coming in your immediate future. The prophet complained many times to God and poured out his painful feelings in lament and prayer.

Sometimes, our feelings of hopelessness may be caused by misconceptions about God and the spiritual reality. Our hopelessness can drive us to examine these beliefs in the light of God's eternal truths and to readjust them.

Consider the dilemma of the prophet Jeremiah and God's response to his anguish. Jeremiah struggled to reconcile his faith and the knowledge of God with what was happening and what was about to happen. This is the inextricable dilemma that all believers inevitably face sooner or later.

In Jeremiah chapter 15, we find the prophet at rock bottom. He bemoaned himself, his fate, and his wounds as deep and incurable. Jeremiah expressed his doubts and suspicions regarding God, comparing him with a deceptive brook and a spring that fails. God answered him and gave him the key to break free:

> "If you return and give up this mistaken tone of distrust and despair, then I will give you again a settled place of quiet and safety, and you will be my minister. If you separate the precious from the vile, cleansing your own heart from unworthy and unwarranted suspicions concerning God's faithfulness, you shall be my mouthpiece for I am with you to save and deliver you" (Jer. 15:19 AMP).

God didn't want Jeremiah to continue to feel hopeless. He invited the prophet to examine his deepest thoughts about his faithfulness and return to peace and safety.

Hopelessness is God's invitation for us to give up some of the following misconceptions:

- The belief that we are justified in feeling offended and hurt. Whether we perceive ourselves as a victim depends on us, not on our circumstances.
- The attitude of mistrust and suspicion concerning God and his faithfulness. It is important to understand that these suspicions are unfounded and unworthy. Because God, his character, and his Word are unchanging, he is and always remains faithful to himself and his promises. His faithfulness is the unshakable foundation of our hope.
- The attitude of despair and the reluctance to believe that healing is possible, as well as the unwillingness to take a step in that direction.
- Our limited perspective on our situation. Too often we focus on the visible, material, short-term things of life that are little to no value. Let's not forget that we see only a microscopic part of the whole, while God sees the beginning and the end and the entire story in-between.

If you are harboring similar attitudes and opinions, here are some truths to focus on instead:
- God is good. On that fact, we can base our expectation to see and experience his goodness in our lives. (Ps. 100:4-5)
- There is no hopeless situation! The hopeless situation excludes God and spiritual reality. And since it is impossible to exclude God, who is the cause, the center, and the meaning of everything, we can have hope in every situation. (1 Pet. 1:3)
- The hope of Christ is always present, even when our expectations aren't met. This is the hope of full restoration and redemption of all creation.(Acts 3:21)
- When we experience difficulties, the Holy Spirit is producing eternal fruit within us. These are the fruits of endurance, kindness, self-control, and much more. (Gal. 5:22-23)

God is more concerned with resolving internal conflicts than with external ones.[17] In his response to Jeremiah, he promises us several things when we take responsibility for our thinking. They relate to the improvement of our mental state and our ability to serve him. God promises us lasting peace of mind and tranquility. Is there anything more valuable and wonderful than that? But he also promises to be our safety and to lead us to freedom from anxiety and various kinds of fears. He increases our capacity to serve him. Lastly, God imparts to us divine wisdom: the ability to see his perspective and will for us, and to speak with his words. All this gives us the strength to live the lives we are created for.

How God Lifts Us from the Pit of Despair
There are many biblical examples of godly people sinking to the bottom of the muddy pit of hopelessness and despair. But God never left them there when they cried out to him. He used their painful experience to strengthen their faith, to let them experience more of his healing and comfort, and to mature their character.

Psalm 40, for example, tells a story of King David coming out of the pit of despair. David surely had many reasons to feel hopeless, discouraged, and depressed at times. In between receiving God's promises and seeing them come to fulfillment, he spent years running, hiding, and surviving. His life was constantly in danger. He lived like an outlaw. It seemed that instead of coming closer to the promise, it grew more distant and impossible. David faced immense opposition, betrayal, fights, and hardships.
But in Psalm 40, he shares:

> "I waited patiently for the Lord; he turned to me and heard my cry. He lifted me out of the slimy pit, out of the mud and mire; he set my feet on a rock and gave me a firm place to stand. He put a new song in my mouth, a hymn of praise to our God. Many

---

[17] James 1:2-4, 1 Peter 1:6, James 1:12, 1 Peter 5:10

will see and fear the Lord and put their trust in him" (Psalm 40:1-3).

In his despair, David continued to wait patiently for the Lord. During this time of waiting and trusting, the Lord lifted him up out of the mud and mire and gave him a firm footing.

Mud and mire describe accurately the feeling of total helplessness we feel when we are stuck in depression. We need someone bigger and stronger than ourselves to pull us out of the sticky, suffocating mud and place us on firm and stable ground. To be able to stand denotes a level of resilience, stronger faith, and a deeper connection with God. But God didn't stop there—he gave David a new song. It is difficult to sing when we feel hopeless and depressed.

Only God is able to change the melody in our hearts from mourning to joy, from hopelessness to praise, as he promises here:

> "And provide for those who grieve in Zion—to bestow on them a crown of beauty instead of ashes, the oil of joy instead of mourning, and a garment of praise instead of a spirit of despair. They will be called oaks of righteousness, a planting of the Lord for the display of his splendor" (Isa. 61:3).

Such a glorious exchange and transformation!

When Jesus Christ started his ministry in Luke 4, these words from the prophet Isaiah were his opening statement. Yes, we will sit in ashes, we will mourn, and we will despair, even to the point of death. But with our Lord and through the power of the Holy Spirit, we will come out of this darkness adorned with precious jewels. We will emerge with the treasure of eternal beauty, joy, praise, and righteousness, reflecting God's glory. Our lives will become a testimony and will lead others to put their trust in the Lord.

Declarations

- Hopelessness and depression can be transformed into godly sorrow and lead me to repentance and submission to God.
- Depression often paves the way for me to return to God and reconnect with Him.
- God can use hopelessness and depression as tools to test my beliefs and the foundation of my faith.
- Hopelessness can push me to fix my misconceptions about God.
- Only God is able to change the melody in my heart from mourning and hopelessness to joy, praise, and renewed hope.

Losses and Gains

Losses When I Face Hopelessness
1. The loss of hope for a better present and future
2. The loss of the expectation for good things to happen
3. The loss of the expectation for God to deliver me or the people I love
4. The loss of joy and satisfaction
5. The loss of motivation and the desire to live, grow, and change
6. The loss of trust in God

Gains When I Draw Near to God
1. The gain of a tested and perfected faith
2. The gain of a new, eternal perspective
3. The gain of spiritual and emotional growth and maturity
4. The gain of compassion and empathy
5. The gain of learning to put my hope in God

6. The gain of learning to use my spiritual eyes
7. The gain of God's comfort
8. The gain of examining my beliefs and changing them to match God's truths
9. The gain of a new level of God's deliverance and healing
10. The gain of knowing God as the God of restoration and resurrection
11. The gain of learning to wait on the Lord

Reflection Questions

1. Have you struggled with hopelessness or depression? What was the reason?
2. Has your struggle with depression brought you closer to God? How?

Meditation Verses

"He will wipe every tear from their eyes. There will be no more death or mourning or crying or pain, for the old order of things has passed away" (Rev. 21:4).

"Godly sorrow brings repentance that leads to salvation and leaves no regret, but worldly sorrow brings death" (2 Cor. 7:10).

"If you return and give up this mistaken tone of distrust and despair, then I will give you again a settled place of quiet and safety, and you will be my minister. If you separate the precious from the vile, cleansing your own heart from unworthy and unwarranted suspicions concerning God's faithfulness, you shall be my mouthpiece for I am with you to save and deliver you" (Jer. 15:19 AMP).

"I waited patiently for the Lord; he turned to me and heard my cry. He lifted me out of the slimy pit, out of the mud and mire; he set my feet on a rock and gave me a firm place to stand. He put a new song in my mouth, a hymn of praise to our God. Many will see and fear the Lord and put their trust in him" (Ps. 40:1-3).

"And provide for those who grieve in Zion—to bestow on them a crown of beauty instead of ashes, the oil of joy instead of mourning, and a garment of praise instead of a spirit of despair. They will be called oaks of righteousness, a planting of the Lord for the display of his splendor" (Isa. 61:3).

Prayer

Dear Lord,

I am sinking in the mud and mire of hopelessness and depression. I am losing my motivation to live, grow and change. It is difficult to expect anything good. I see only blackness when I try to imagine my future.

Lord, you know why I am sitting in this pit. I am completely helpless to pull myself out. I cry out to you. Help me wait patiently for your deliverance and healing and plant my feet on firm ground.

Show me any misconceptions I am harboring about you that may nurture my hopelessness. Help me renew my mind and transform my thinking through your eternal truths.

Strengthen my faith and boost my hope. Give me unshakable hope, firmly rooted in you, not in my circumstances and not in my abilities.

Lord, I know you have good plans and have prepared a glorious future for me and all who love you. I declare your goodness and faithfulness now and put my trust in you.

In Jesus' name. Amen.

12

The Gifts Hidden in Failure

I am sitting on the couch and here it comes again: the tension in my body and the craving for instant relief. It is just an ordinary day.

I start looking for a book, and my hands just happen to pick up one on marriage that my husband and I used to read together. There, tucked between the pages, is a sheet of paper written by both of us. On the first half of the page, he had written the things he was committing to in our marriage, and on the other half I wrote my commitments. Looking at his handwriting stabs my heart. Memories come back to life. Memories are the only thing I have now.

I go about my day, working on my daily tasks and worrying about problems and relationships. My neck becomes stiff from sitting at the computer, and my body aches.

Finally, it's time to rest. I want to watch a movie to distract myself—it happens to be a romantic drama, a story of shared love, passion, and longing. Again, I feel this cold emptiness in my chest that screams to be filled. My body is tense, my soul is aching.

It is just a normal day, but I want relief and I want it now. A thought enters my mind for a second: "You don't need this, don't do it, it will not help you." I dismiss it. "I want this, I need relief."

Before this internal dialogue continues, I get up and go to the kitchen. I open the cupboards, grab a tray, and load it with anything I can find: cookies, chocolates, nuts, crackers. I go back into the living room and my indulgence begins.

Guess how I feel after that? Not better.

On the contrary, my stomach is full to the point of throwing up, and my soul faces another kind of pain: the pain of failure, shame, and self-condemnation. Thoughts flood my mind like muddy torrents.

> *You did it again. You are such a failure.*
> *You will never overcome this. You will never break this cycle.*
> *You could have turned to God for comfort and strength, but you deliberately chose not to.*
> *You failed again.*
> *There is no hope for you.*
> *How can you serve God when you fail, again and again?*

I'm sure you're familiar with similar thoughts, because all of us have failed. We all know how it feels to fail, and the kind of messages it broadcasts. It seems failure has accompanied us since our childhood. We fail to:

- be good and obedient children
- behave
- have good grades in school
- meet our parents' and teachers' expectations
- meet the current beauty standard
- be accepted and loved by everyone
- pass exams
- land a good job
- be the best parents
- be the spouse our partner expects and needs
- live holy lives and please God
- do God's will all the time
- accomplish a goal or a dream

And the list goes on. It seems our lives are made up of a series of failures and we should be used to it by now. Nevertheless, failure is a painful experience because it leads to losses, which can negatively affect how we view ourselves and God.

When I think of my failures, the ones that hurt the most are the ones connected to those closest to me, the people I love. It hurts the most when I fail to love my family and friends the way they need me to. It hurts the most when I fail God.

I feel like a failure whenever I lash out with angry or unrestrained words, when I am too critical and judgmental, or whenever I harden my heart and refuse to forgive. I feel like a failure when I look for comfort in food, indulging myself in chocolate and sweets, trying to suppress the pain and emptiness I feel.

Every time I turn to other things for comfort and avoid turning to God instead, I fail.

Why is it so painful, and what does it mean to fail?

A common definition for failure is a lack of success, non-fulfillment, defeat, or the neglect or omission of expected or required action. According to the Merriam-Webster dictionary, failure carries several meanings like "an omission of occurrence or performance, a state of inability to perform a normal function, a fracturing or giving way under stress, lack of success, or a falling short."[18] What are our losses when we don't have success and fall short?

Our Losses When We Face a Failure

God wired us to want to do the right thing and to succeed. Especially when we become Christians, the Holy Spirit works in us to desire God's will and to empower us to carry it out. "For it is God who works in you to will and to act in order to fulfill his good purpose" (Phil. 2:13).

---

[18] https://www.merriam-webster.com/dictionary/failure

So, the lack of success, which is the essence of failure, strikes our self-perception and self-confidence. Shame and guilt are powerful emotions and may lead to losing our self-validation. This means we don't feel worthy and have difficulty respecting ourselves. We begin to believe our failures make us unworthy.

The omission to do what we know we ought to do and failure to achieve a goal, desire, or dream, may also lead to a loss of self-fulfillment, satisfaction, and contentment. The Bible says that "hope deferred makes the heart sick, but a longing fulfilled is a tree of life" (Prov. 13:12).

It is only natural to feel sad, discouraged, and even depressed when we fail at things we long for. This may also lead to losing motivation, enthusiasm, and willingness to get up, move forward, and seek healing and restoration.

Other losses directly stemming from failure we may experience are in the sphere of our relationships. Due to failure in our work, business, and ministries, or in our personal lives, we may lose other people's respect, approval, and admiration. We can even lose a relationship because of failure or what the other person perceives as a failure.

Finally, one of the heaviest and most tragic losses that failure may bring is losing our close fellowship with God and turning our backs on him. These are serious losses with far-reaching consequences.

So why does God allow it? What is failure teaching us? What are the gifts and blessings of failure?

Learning to Depend on God and His grace

There is one interesting thing about failure: we usually fail in the area we feel the strongest. The reason for that is that when we feel strong, we often slip into self-reliance and forget to rely on God's grace.

For example, I kept returning to my bad habit of misusing food for comfort in the same area where I felt settled and strong—the area of my health and well-being. My usual pattern is one of self-discipline, a healthy diet, and exercise. I know what is good for me and what is not. Eating moderately and healthy is a way of life for me. However, it is exactly here where I am often failing.

There are a lot of examples in the Bible of people of faith who failed in an area in which they were strong. That's why God's Word warns us: "So, if you think you are standing firm, be careful that you don't fall!" (1 Cor. 10:12)

Let's start with Abraham, who is known for his faith. By faith, Abraham left his homeland and followed God into the unknown. And yet, a little later, we find him in Egypt, where he failed to trust God for protection. Out of fear that the Egyptians might take his life to get to his beautiful wife, Sarah, he lied about her, saying she was his sister. This led to a colossal disaster. (Gen. 12)

Then we meet another hero of faith—Moses. This is how the Bible describes his character: "Now Moses was a very humble man, more humble than anyone else on the face of the earth" (Num. 12:3). He was established and strong in his humility.

But we also learn that Moses killed an Egyptian in his outrage. (Exod. 2:11-12) There was a more serious failure, too. In his anger, this most humble man disobeyed God and didn't follow his instructions to speak to the rock. Instead, he struck it twice. (Num. 20:7-12) Unfortunately, this led to dire consequences for him—God didn't allow him to enter the Promised Land.

We see this pattern of failure in the entire history of God's chosen people, too. Precisely because they were God's chosen people, they felt strong in their special covenant relationship with God. But this was also their weakest spot. They failed multiple times to follow God and obey his law and commands. Psalm 78 depicts this cycle of failing and returning vividly.

> "Their hearts were not loyal to him, they were not faithful to his covenant. Yet he was merciful; he forgave their iniquities and did

not destroy them. Time after time, he restrained his anger and did not stir up his full wrath. He remembered that they were but flesh, a passing breeze that does not return" (Ps. 78:37-39).

In the New Testament, we find Peter, who felt too strong and overconfident as a disciple and follower of Jesus. He was the first disciple to confess Jesus as the Messiah. (Matt. 16:16) However, he relied on his ability to follow Jesus, so it was shocking and soul-shattering when he denied the Lord three times, exactly as Jesus predicted. (Luke 22:54-62)

These examples teach us that failure can have this fantastic ability of breaking our self-reliance and self-dependency. From this humble and needy position, we start learning to depend on God and his grace. We train ourselves to acknowledge our weaknesses and invite God's power into them. Failure propels us to experience his grace as sufficient. It shows us what it means to be empowered by God, to be plugged into a greater source of strength outside ourselves. Only then is it possible to live out this paradox of being weak and strong at the same time so beautifully described by the Apostle Paul.

> "But he said to me, "My grace is sufficient for you, for my power is made perfect in weakness." Therefore I will boast all the more gladly about my weaknesses, so that Christ's power may rest on me. That is why, for Christ's sake, I delight in weaknesses, in insults, in hardships, in persecutions, in difficulties. For when I am weak, then I am strong" (2 Co. 12:9-10).

We can truly boast in our weakness because then we are relying on God's strength, and this makes all the difference. It is actually beneficial to feel weak because we can depend on him and boast with him, leaning on his strength every step of the way. In this way, we get to know him deeper and deeper.

Learning to Practice Repentance and Accept Forgiveness

This is one of the most precious benefits and blessings of failure. Everybody knows how difficult it is to accept God's forgiveness when we fail. The guilt, shame, self-condemnation, and self-accusation packed with powerful emotions and internal narratives are huge stumbling blocks on the path to healing and restoration.

Here is what God wants us to know: "For though the righteous fall seven times, they rise again, but the wicked stumble when calamity strikes" (Prov. 24:16).

God expects us to rise again and move forward. Not only that, but he has provided everything we need to make this possible.

Once we confess our failure, the Lord is ready to heal us from the wound of failure and make us grow in knowing him and his love. "If we confess our sins, he is faithful and just and will forgive us our sins and purify us from all unrighteousness" (1 John 1:9).

We see this beautifully illustrated in the story of Peter's repentance and restoration. There is one emotionally loaded and transformational moment for Peter after his failure, described by the evangelist Luke: "The Lord turned and looked straight at Peter. Then Peter remembered the word the Lord had spoken to him: 'Before the rooster crows today, you will disown me three times.' And he went outside and wept bitterly" (Luke 22:61-62).

What was this look? Was it a look of judgment, a kind of "I told you so" look? No, I believe this was a look full of pain, but also flooded with compassion, understanding, deep empathy, limitless love, and acceptance.

It is not God's judgment and anger that brings us back to him, but it is the revelation of his unfathomable and unconditional love. A love that is present all the time; when we fail, and when we succeed; when we are strong, and when we are weak; when we are far from him, and when we are near.

It is a look that conveys, "Nothing you did and will do can make me love you less. Trust my love and my willingness to restore and heal you. Come back to me."

Friend, next time you fail, picture Jesus looking at you this way and trust his unconditional love and acceptance. This will help you accept his invitation for restoration.

We need time to weep for our failures, but we need also to move forward and accept God's healing grace. This is what Peter did when he allowed Jesus to minister to him and build him up after his failure. (John 21:15-19)

This was such an intimate and profound moment for Peter. He trusted Jesus as his lord, healer, and restorer, and Jesus publicly trusted Peter again to be his servant despite his failure.

It was as if Jesus was saying: "Your failure didn't disqualify you. Ultimately, it is not up to you. I am partnering with you. My grace is working with you. Together, we will make it. I trust you."

Jesus was rebuilding Peter's confidence, but this time, this was not self-confidence. No, it was God-confidence. He can do the same for us.

We shouldn't avoid failure, we should embrace it. Without failure, there is no true success. It is a brilliant teacher, exposing the condition and motivations of our hearts and keeping us on the path of humility. It is a necessary instrument in God's arsenal of training and preparation tools for spiritual growth.

Declarations

- Failure can break my self-reliance and self-dependency. This is good.
- God's grace is sufficient in my weakness.
- I can boast about my weakness because then I am relying on God's strength.

- Failure is not permanent and doesn't change God's love and acceptance of me.
- God expects me to rise again and move forward after I failed.

Losses and Gains

Losses When I Face Failure
1. The loss of self-confidence and self-validation
2. The loss of self-respect
3. The loss of satisfaction and contentment
4. The loss of motivation, enthusiasm, and the willingness to get up, move forward
5. The loss of other people's respect, approval, and admiration
6. The loss of a relationship

Gains When I Draw Near to God
1. The gain of spiritual growth and maturity
2. The gain of experiencing and trusting God's unconditional love and acceptance in Christ
3. The gain of humility and dying to self
4. The gain of learning to depend on God and boast in him
5. The gain of repentance and accepting God's forgiveness
6. The gain of finding God's strength in my weaknesses
7. The gain of finding self-validation and realization in God
8. The gain of experiencing God's willingness to forgive, heal, and restore
9. The gain of of tested and purified motivation
10. The gain of of growing in perseverance, self-discipline, and patience
11. The gain of becoming stronger and more resilient
12. The gain of aligning my concept for success with what the Word of God says about success

Reflection Questions

1. What is the one area of life you feel you fail the most in? Why? Are there any failures you need to accept God'' forgiveness for? Which ones?
2. Which of these benefits of failure have you experienced in your life?

Meditation Verses

"For it is God who works in you to will and to act in order to fulfill his good purpose" (Phil. 2:13).

"So, if you think you are standing firm, be careful that you don't fall!" (1 Cor. 10:12)

"But he said to me, "My grace is sufficient for you, for my power is made perfect in weakness." Therefore I will boast all the more gladly about my weaknesses, so that Christ's power may rest on me. That is why, for Christ's sake, I delight in weaknesses, in insults, in hardships, in persecutions, in difficulties. For when I am weak, then I am strong" (2 Cor. 12:9-10).

"For though the righteous fall seven times, they rise again, but the wicked stumble when calamity strikes" (Prov. 24:16).

"If we confess our sins, he is faithful and just and will forgive us our sins and purify us from all unrighteousness" (1 John 1:9).

"It does not, therefore, depend on human desire or effort, but on God's mercy" (Rom. 9:16).

Prayer

Dear Lord,

I have failed in so many ways and so many areas of my life. I have the feeling I have failed you and this hurts. Help me disentangle the lies of failure and free me from the feelings of guilt, shame, and self-condemnation.

Fill me with the courage to receive your forgiveness, healing, and restoration and to move forward. I don't want to get stuck, Lord. Help me trust your unconditional love again. Your love doesn't depend on my failures or achievements.

Help me humble myself and learn to rely on your strength and mercy in everything. Let me experience your healing and restoration in the wounded places of my heart.

In Jesus' name. Amen.

13

The Gifts Hidden in Pain

Being human means experiencing pain—emotional, physical, mental, and spiritual. Pain comes in different manifestations and intensity, and it is our constant companion from birth to grave. That's why we need to learn to view and handle our pain properly and let them pull us closer to God. Some of the best gifts come when our lives are wrapped in pain.

My earliest memories of unbearable pain are from my childhood and teenage years. I lived with a monster who inflicted physical, mental, and emotional pain regularly, although unpredictably. This was the monster of alcoholism and violence that had taken hold of my father. This evil tormented and abused all members of our family, destroying our feelings of safety, protection, and worthiness. Fear and shame engulfed me. I became acquainted with gut-wrenching pain.

> *Pain in my body when he hit me.*
> *Pain in my soul when he humiliated me.*
> *Pain in my spirit when he took away my hope.*

Pain was like a dark serum that flooded my veins and filled my heart. It was a poisonous mixture of shame, unworthiness, fear, hopelessness, utter helplessness, and despair. The claws of pain made me question my existence and drove me to suicidal thoughts. I was dying on the inside.

I didn't know that it was so painful to be human. However, what brought me the greatest pain was not the monster in my father, it was discovering that there was a monster in me, too. It shocked me to see glimpses of the evil in my heart—streaks of hatred, bitterness, resentment, anger, unforgiveness, impurity, lack of self-control, and chaos. I didn't know how to remove this suffocating burden, and I felt helpless to do it. My strongest, and yet unattainable, desire was to be good and do good, to love and be loved. The inherent desire of every human, I guess.

But wait. Was this all?

Pain made me feel my humanity to the point I despised it. It stripped me naked and made me feel at my weakest: too weak to bear the pain, too weak to continue living, too weak to deal with the sin and brokenness. But this was also pain's greatest gift.

When we are in pain and at our weakest, our need for God, his strength, and his love is the greatest. These core needs surface from the bottom of our hearts and demand our full attention. Then, we cry out to God. We bow our heads and admit we are just humans who need him more than bread, more than water, and more than our next breath. We need God to live and stop walking around like the living dead.

We need God's grace and strength. Only this is enough to carry us through our greatest pain, because we can do all this through him who gives us strength. (Phil. 4:13)

And when our flesh and heart fail, God remains the strength of our hearts and our portion forever. (Ps 73:26)

I cried out to God, too. I didn't know him, but I knew I needed Him. He answered my soul cry, birthed from the pain, and we started a journey together. Since then, he has led me on a journey of trust, freedom, and transformation. I found life, love, and strength to carry on.

I'm sure you are well acquainted with pain and the losses it brings, too. Often, when we are in pain, we lose our self-control and give ourselves a free pass to do things we know are the wrong choices. But we want quick relief and we use pain as an excuse.

I know this well. For years, I used the pain I went through as an excuse for developing eating disorders, hanging out with bad company, and making unwise and unhealthy choices.

We lose satisfaction, contentment, and our sense of well-being. Even the slightest physical pain, like cutting our finger, brings constant discomfort to the whole body and affects our mood. Pain may make us question our value, worthiness, and lovability.

Pain brings losses, but pain is also our answer to real or perceived losses. When we lose something or someone that we deem precious, we experience pain. Losing something, whether it's our health, a person, a dream, our hopes, or our job, causes us pain.

So, how can we handle pain in a way that can help us unpack its benefits and blessings? What is our pain trying to teach us?

An Invitation to Grow and Change Our Perspective

As believers, when we are in pain, we usually ask a lot of questions. What are we to make of our situation? Doesn't God love us anymore? Does he want to punish us for something? No, quite the opposite is the case.

The Lord loves us and wants to bless us with good beyond our imagination. The highest good he could bless us with is himself and the precious gift of deeper fellowship and intimacy with him. Compared to all other things and people we desire and will eventually lose, this is something we will never lose and can enjoy forever.

We need to adjust our perspective if we are going to endure pain with patience and get out of the pit. Pits, lion's dens, blazing fires, shipwrecks—they all have something in common. They expose our greatest fears and our lesser loves. We are stripped of our greatest fears and our lesser loves.

Suffering and pain force us to grow in the purest form of fear, the fear of the Lord, and to invest in our greatest love—the love for God and all things he holds in high esteem.

There are three ways or spiritual disciplines that help us cooperate with God's purpose for growth and spiritual formation in a season of pain. These are: directing our hopes to God's prophetic vision and promises, the discipline of lamenting, and the discipline of rejoicing in the Lord.

A huge part of our suffering comes from unmet expectations and deferred hopes. We long for something and we have a preconceived idea of how God will meet our needs or what the desired outcome will look like. It is natural to feel disappointed, and even betrayed, when God does not follow our script.

Let's remember that God is good at being God and decide to humble ourselves. We can't tame God, and it is not wise to predict his actions. However, it is wise to direct our hopes for a better world to God's prophetic vision and promises revealed in his word. This is hope for which we have a guarantee.

The second spiritual discipline is learning to lament. Lamenting is expressing our pain and sorrow while remaining hopeful. It is grieving in another way, "not like the rest of mankind, who have no hope" (1 Thess. 4:13).

Lamentations are a gift in our inexpressible struggles—a way to reconcile our pain with our faith, to give a voice to our suffering, yet still hang on to our faith. The tears we shed are precious rain for growing deeper roots. We need both the rain of blessings and the rain of tears if we are to spread deeper roots in Christ, our eternal Rock.

God's Word is also full of exhortations to rejoice in the Lord, to rejoice always, to rejoice in various troubles and trials. Joy is the healthy nutrient we need to grow. We practice joy when we consciously yield to God and let ourselves be rejuvenated and refreshed constantly in his presence.

We can rejoice in the Lord when we choose to focus on him instead of our circumstances. Giving thanks for the smallest things during our day and finding time to worship and praise are means to cultivate joy.

We grow the most in our season of pain when we are nourished by the joys of righteous life and the intimate fellowship with the Lord. "Light shines on the righteous and joy on the upright in heart. Rejoice in the Lord, you who are righteous, and praise his holy name" (Ps. 91:11-12).

The Fruit of Pain and Suffering

Our pain is not in vain, and it has a purpose when placed in God's hands. It will produce a fruit of blessings. The essence of this fruit is becoming more like Christ.

We see all these truths beautifully illustrated in the names of Job's daughters that God gave him after the crushing loss of all his children. We can see three specific blessings after suffering displayed in the names of Job's daughters.

A righteous person, Job lost his fortune, his children, and his health in a brief period. The book of Job in the Bible depicts his physical and emotional suffering and pain after his losses. Also, it gives us a glimpse into his struggle to keep his faith and trust in God despite his circumstances.

Does this story have a happy ending?

Yes, in the last chapter, we read that "God blessed the latter part of Job's life more than the former part" (Job 42:12).

> "And he also had seven sons and three daughters. The first daughter he named Jemimah, the second Keziah, and the third Keren-Happuch. Nowhere in all the land were there found women as beautiful as Job's daughters, and their father granted them an inheritance along with their brothers" (Job 42:13-15).

The Hebrew word "Jemimah" means "dove" and "daylight."[19] The dove is a symbol of the work of the Holy Spirit in the heart and

---

[19] https://www.abarim-publications.com/Meaning/Jemimah.html

mind of the believer. This work brings peace, healing, and hope.

It also helps us walk into the light. Pain and suffering exert pressure on our hearts and force us to open up and bring deep underlying issues to the light. These are usually things that hinder us from becoming whole and mature and loving God and others well.

The first fruit and blessing of our suffering is to experience the transformative and healing power of the Holy Spirit.

The second daughter's name is Keziah. This name has several meanings in Hebrew. The first meaning is "scraped off, ended, cut off."[20] It denotes the end of the suffering and the trial. But it also reminds us of Jesus' atoning sacrifice that reconciled us with God. It reminds us that "It is finished!" (John 19:30)

The word "Keziah" is also related to "cassia," which is a sweet, smelly cinnamon powder. It symbolizes the sweetness of God's nearness, intimate fellowship, and comfort. It is also one of the specific aromas of Jesus. According to Psalm 45 (a wedding song), his clothes smell like cassia.

"All your robes are fragrant with myrrh and aloes and cassia; from palaces adorned with ivory the music of the strings makes you glad" (Ps. 45:8).

The second blessing and fruit of our suffering is experiencing the intimate nearness of God's loving presence and being saturated in the aroma of Christ.

The name of Job's third daughter, "Keren–Happuch," has several meanings in Hebrew: "a beautifier, to radiate with beautiful eyes, and having horns (strength)."[21]

This illustrates how, as a fruit of our suffering, we become more like Christ, displaying his beauty, glory, and power in our lives. Besides, going through suffering and trials strengthens us, making us resilient and stable.

---

[20] https://www.abarim-publications.com/Meaning/Keziah.html
[21] https://www.abarim-publications.com/Meaning/Keren-happuch.html

The third blessing is the blessing of experiencing and reflecting God's beauty and power, so we can fulfill the calling to shine like stars.

"So that you may become blameless and pure, 'children of God without fault in a warped and crooked generation.' Then you will shine among them like stars in the sky as you hold firmly to the word of life" (Phil. 2:15-16).

This study of the names of Job's daughters shows us that the essence of the fruit of our pain and suffering is being formed into the image of Christ.

First, we experience healing and peace through the work of the Holy Spirit and the hope of a new beginning.

Then we let the Spirit adorn us, beautify us, and soak us in the aromas of Christ.

In this way, we become beautiful, radiating God's glory and beauty and displaying his power in our lives.

How Jesus Handled His Greatest Pain

When I think of intense pain and agony, I often think of our Lord Jesus Christ and his struggle in Gethsemane. He endured inexplicable pain and suffering at the cross, but the true agony of the soul was in Gethsemane. There, Jesus pleaded with his Father to be spared from this ultimate physical and spiritual pain.

The struggle at Gethsemane reveals Jesus' humanity to the fullest. It also gives us a powerful example of how to handle our greatest pains so they can become the birthplace of God's best plans and purposes.

Jesus expressed his pain to his trusted friends and God in prayer. He didn't hide anything. He laid his heart bare, letting the crushing pain surface.

Then he said to them, "My soul is overwhelmed with sorrow to the point of death. Stay here and keep watch with me" (Matt. 26:38).

Jesus asked God to spare him from the pain and suffering, but he placed God's will above this desire.

"Going a little farther, he fell with his face to the ground and prayed, 'My Father, if it is possible, may this cup be taken from me. Yet not as I will, but as you will'" (Matt. 26:39).

Can we do this, too? Are we able to come to God with our pain but desire his will more? Can we trust that his will is always good for us, even if it includes going through excruciating pain and suffering? Can we humble ourselves to the point of death—the death of our weaknesses and humanity?

God denied Jesus' prayer. And we praise him for this "no" even now. Jesus' cup of suffering was and is the greatest gift to all people.

Although God said no in Gethsemane, he didn't leave Jesus while his heart was breaking into pieces. God sent heavenly help, supernatural strength, and comfort.

"An angel from heaven appeared to him and strengthened him" (Luke 22:43).

We are never alone in our pain. God cares deeply, especially in the moments when his best will is not to remove the pain until it accomplishes its purposes in us. We are connected to the Source of all strength and power in the universe. That's why we can embrace our weakness and cling to his strength.

We should not be afraid when pain threatens to destroy us. We can submit to God and allow him to raise us again in his strength, love, and peace. When we die the death of our own weakness, we live again in the strength and beauty of a life with purpose.

Declarations

- Some of the best gifts are wrapped in pain.
- God can use my pain to restore me to a life of purpose.
- Pain intensifies my need for God so I can experience more of him.
- Pain teaches me to embrace my weaknesses and cling to God's strength.
- Pain forces me to grow in the fear of the Lord and to invest in the love for God and all things he holds in high esteem.

Losses and Gains

Losses When I Face Pain
1. The loss of self-control
2. The loss of physical and emotional well-being
3. The loss of satisfaction and contentment in the area of pain
4. The loss of peace
5. The loss of hope for healing

Gains When I Draw Near to God
1. The gain of clinging to God's strength
2. The gain of accepting our weaknesses and limitations
3. The gain of receiving God's comfort and compassion
4. The gain of developing compassion and empathy
5. The gain of spiritual and emotional growth and maturity
6. The gain of spiritual, mental, and emotional transformation
7. The gain of learning soul-care
8. The gain of experiencing God's restoration and resurrection to a life of purpose
9. The gain of a new level of God's deliverance and healing

10. The gain of intensified longing for God
11. The gain of perfected faith and testimony
12. The gain of displaying more of God's beauty, glory, and power

Reflection Questions

1. How do you handle emotional pain?
2. Have you received a gift from God wrapped in pain?

Meditation Verses

"My flesh and my heart may fail, but God is the strength of my heart and my portion forever" (Ps. 73:26).

"Brothers and sisters, we do not want you to be uninformed about those who sleep in death, so that you do not grieve like the rest of mankind, who have no hope" (1 Thess. 4:13).

"God blessed the latter part of Job's life more than the former part" (Job 42:12).

"As you know, we count as blessed those who have persevered. You have heard of Job's perseverance and have seen what the Lord finally brought about. The Lord is full of compassion and mercy" (James 5:11)

"'My Father, if it is possible, may this cup be taken from me. Yet not as I will, but as you will'" (Matt. 26:39).

"An angel from heaven appeared to him and strengthened him" (Luke 22:43).

"So that you may become blameless and pure, 'children of God without fault in a warped and crooked generation.' Then you will shine among them like stars in the sky as you hold firmly to the word of life" (Phil. 2:15-16).

"He gives strength to the weary and increases the power of the weak. Those who hope in the Lord will renew their strength. They will soar on wings like eagles; they will run and not grow weary, they will walk and not be faint" (Isa. 40:29, 31).

Prayer

Dear Lord,

I am in pain. My soul hurts, my body aches. I come to you to express my pain and hand it over to you.

Take away my pain and heal me. Use my pain for good and bring purpose out of this pain. Let my suffering be not in vain.

I am just a weak vessel, and I need you desperately. I need your grace, healing, and strength to carry on. I declare that your grace is sufficient to cover my weaknesses, limitations, and pains. Show yourself strong on my behalf.

Take away this cup of suffering from me, yet not as I will, but as you will. I want your will above all, Lord.

In Jesus' name. Amen.

The End

Summary of Declarations

Chapter One: The Gifts Hidden in Adversity

- Adversity trains my faith muscles and helps me grow spiritually, become mature, and be able to carry heavier loads without breaking.
- Adversity is part of God's special preparation and training for his kingdom.
- God loves me and he wants to bless me in and through adversity.
- God will infuse me with strength and will help me in every situation.
- Unmet expectations are designed to propel me closer to God, to enable me "to grasp how wide and long and high and deep is the love of Christ" (Eph. 3:18).

Chapter Two: The Gifts Hidden in Sadness

- Even though I am stricken with sadness and sorrow, even though I am afflicted, I will rejoice in the Lord. I will rejoice in his love, in his character, in hs promises, and in his presence.
- In my sorrow, I have access to a greater, higher joy based on the fact that God is always with me and he works tirelessly in me, through me, and for me.
- My sorrow opens the door to experience God as the God of

all comfort and compassion.
- Even if I may lose my temporary hope, I still have my constant, personified hope in Christ.
- In my sadness, the Lord is there—knowing, feeling, holding, comforting, and working.

Chapter Three: The Gifts Hidden in Anxiety

- I give God the freedom to do as he sees fit with me because this is the safest choice I can make.
- God has only my good in mind because I belong to him. God has done and always does what is best for me (from an eternal perspective) and what is best for his glory.
- Everything that happens to me is right in its place, is best for me, is at the right moment, and is done in the best way for me to grow. Everything is guided by the loving hand of God.
- I choose not to resist God's ways and not to fight against my true self.

Chapter Four: The Gifts Hidden in Rejection

- I know and rely on God's love.
- God is the lover of my soul, my ultimate satisfier, and the source of all my blessings.
- My value as a person is not dependent on my accomplishments and success. God continued to love me before and after the rejection of my work.
- Very often, rejection is God's way of protection and redirection in my life.
- God sees me and loves me always. I am valuable to him.

Chapter Five: The Gifts Hidden in Loneliness

- I can use solitude and isolation to connect with God and listen to His voice without distractions.
- I may feel lonely, but I am never truly alone.
- God can strengthen and establish my purpose and identity in periods of loneliness and isolation.
- God allows loneliness to prepare me and help me connect deeper with Him.
- Jesus is my constant companion, guide, and best friend.

Chapter Six: The Gifts Hidden in Unmet Expectations

- Unmet expectations are and will be a major part of my life.
- My expectations are an expression of my basic attitudes, ideas, and beliefs. They indicate how I think about myself, life, relationships, marriage, friendship, happiness, God, etc.
- One of the greatest gains of unmet expectations is to learn to depend on God and put my hope in him.
- When I seek and trust God, he promises joy, peace, and satisfaction in all circumstances, regardless of my unmet expectations.
- My happiness is not measured by the number of met expectations or fulfilled desires, but by knowing God's love.

Chapter Seven: The Gifts Hidden in Disillusionment

- Disillusionment is an opportunity to examine my theology and make changes.
- God longs to seal the cracks in my faith foundation with hope, comfort, and renewed strength.

- The goal of every test and trial is to receive more blessings and good from the Lord. It is enlargement and preparation to partake in his glory.
- God always has the last word.

Chapter Eight: The Gifts Hidden in Grief

- When I fail to grieve losses, I miss out on an essential way that God wants to meet me.
- Grief impacts me emotionally, mentally, spiritually, and physically. That's why it is crucial to embrace it and use its healing and transformational potential.
- When I lament and express my grief in the presence of God, I can be myself without a mask.
- The Lord Jesus Christ is my safest person and the ultimate grief expert. He is fully able to empathize because he knows experientially every trial and every kind of suffering.
- Grief can shape me into a comforter, encourager, and mature lover.
- Grief can help me grow in a new measure of freedom.

Chapter Nine: The Gifts Hidden in Betrayal

- God loves me. I choose to trust the reason the betrayal is happening. I trust his plan and purpose.
- I am asking God for help, and I am confident that he will give me what I need.
- I will survive the betrayal and I will thrive because of God's goodness and faithfulness.
- I will draw near to God and allow him to bring all the blessings and gifts hidden in this painful experience.

Chapter Ten: The Gifts Hidden in Broken Dreams

- My dreams are a powerful instrument of self- and God-discovery.
- I submit the fulfillment of my dreams, both how and when they will happen, to God as the giver and fulfiller of dreams.
- Broken dreams are God's way to mend and redirect my heart.
- When my dreams are shattered, God remains sovereign, doing immeasurably more than I can ask for and imagine.
- All my longings, desires, and dreams will find their fulfillment in Christ and his kingdom.

Chapter Eleven: The Gifts Hidden in Hopelessness

- Hopelessness and depression can be transformed into godly sorrow and lead me to repentance and submission to God.
- Depression often paves the way for me to return to God and reconnect with him.
- God can use hopelessness and depression as tools to test my beliefs and the foundation of my faith.
- Hopelessness can push me to fix my misconceptions about God.
- Only God is able to change the melody in my heart from mourning and hopelessness to joy, praise, and renewed hope.

Chapter Twelve: The Gifts Hidden in Failure

- Failure can break my self-reliance and self-dependency. This is good.
- God's grace is sufficient in my weakness.
- I can boast about my weakness because then I am relying on God's strength.

- Failure is not permanent and doesn't change God's love and acceptance of me.
- God expects me to rise again and move forward after I failed.

Chapter Thirteen: The Gifts Hidden in Pain

- Some of the best gifts are wrapped in pain.
- God can use my pain to restore me to a life of purpose.
- Pain intensifies my need for God so I can experience more of him.
- Pain teaches me to embrace my weaknesses and cling to God's strength.
- Pain forces me to grow in the fear of the Lord and to invest in the love for God and all things he holds in high esteem.

A Request from the Author

Thank you for reading *Draw Near: How Painful Experiences Become the Birthplace of Blessings*. I hope you found comfort, hope, encouragement and help for your suffering heart in its pages.

I would love to hear your thoughts about the book. Would you consider taking a moment and sending me a few sentences on how *Draw Near* impacted you? Your comments and feedback mean a lot to me and will help me in serving you better.

Send me your thoughts at hadassah.treu@gmail.com.

Would you consider other suffering hearts, too? Yes, you can help with a simple, honest review.

Could you take a few moments and write a 1-3 sentence review on *Draw Near* and leave it on the site you purchased the book on? And if you want to help even more, you could leave the same review on the *Draw Near* book page on Goodreads. Your review is important and will help others who could benefit from the book. And they will help me, as an author, to produce more quality resources. Thank you!

Warmly,
Hadassah

As a thanks, please accept this gift—a free printable (PDF):
10 Biblical Truths for When Life Doesn't Feel Good
Download yours today!
https://onthewaybg.com/wp-content/uploads/2023/01/10-Biblical-Truths-for-When-Life-Doesnt-Feel-Good.pdf

Acknowledgments

I thank God and my Lord Jesus Christ that he brought me so far and made a dream come true. I wrote my first poem and short stories in rhymes when I was seven, a Bulgarian girl born in a communist country.

You found me when I was seventeen and continued encouraging my gift for writing and learning languages through my teachers. Fast forward over two decades later: you planted a dream in my heart to write about you and for your glory, and I plunged myself into this adventure. You prepared a path for me to grow and mature both as a writer and as your servant.

In 2023, you brought me the perfect partner to birth my first solo book.

Thank you, Lord, because you worked all things together in my life to make me the author of this book. All the painful experiences I went through with you were not in vain because they changed me. Now, I see the fruit of my suffering.

I thank my beloved husband, Thomas, who believed in me wholeheartedly and was my greatest supporter and cheerleader. You were my most precious gift from God in this world. You are part of me, part of this book, and will be part of every book I will write.

I thank my dear friends (what a blessing you are!) and my family members who believed in me and cheered me on.

I am deeply thankful for all my writing friends and supporters, my faithful tribe all over the world. I learned so much from you all and I am blessed to connect, interact, cooperate with you, and serve you. Being part of Proverbs 31 Ministries COMPEL Training played a huge part in my growing as a writer, too.

Thank you to my publisher, Samantha Cabrera, from Calla Press Publishing. It is such a joy working with you. I love your vision for the book and the way you brought it to life.

Finally, thank you to my readers! It is an honor and joy to write for you, to serve you, and to draw you closer to God.

Hadassah Treu

About the Author

Hadassah Treu is an award-winning Christian bilingual blogger, author, poet, and speaker, the Encouraging Blogger Award Winner for 2020. She is a communication specialist and translator, holding a master's in international relations and lives in Bulgaria, Europe.

Hadassah loves to encourage and motivate people to stand firm in the faith, and to grow spiritually by applying biblical truths in their lives. She loves diving deeper into the Word of God and finding hidden treasures.

Hadassah is a regular contributor to the faith-based platforms Devotable, Koinonia, and COMPEL Proverbs 31 Ministries Blog. She has been featured in the Upper Room, (In)courage, Proverbs 31 Ministries, Her View From Home, Living by Design Ministries, Thoughts About God, Aletheia Today, Today's Christian Living, and other popular sites.

Hadassah is also a contributing author to a dozen devotional and poetry anthologies. She is also the author of two poetry books in Bulgarian: "A Guarantee for Another Life" and "Memories Keeper."

Hadassah is no stranger to suffering and losses. With God, she could walk the road of suffering, unfulfilled desires, and unmet expectations to find out that the same road leads to a new purpose, growth, deeper friendship with God, and unexpected blessings. From the platform of her greatest pains equipped with lessons gathered on the way, she delivers a powerful message on how God's love transforms our painful experiences.

Connect with Hadassah here:

https://onthewaybg.com/
https://twitter.com/onthewaybg
https://www.facebook.com/onthewaybg/
https://www.pinterest.at/onthewaybg/
https://www.instagram.com/hadassahtreu/
https://medium.com/@hadassah.treu
https://www.youtube.com/@hadassahtreu-author
https://www.amazon.com/author/hadassah-treu
https://www.goodreads.com/hadassahtreu
https://hadassahtreu.gumroad.com/

Milton Keynes UK
Ingram Content Group UK Ltd.
UKHW042304240324
439966UK00001B/80